MW00873842

How to Fix Your Credit

Learn the secrets the credit industry doesn't want you to know!

S&D Capital Holdings, LLC
2014

First Printing: 2014

ISBN 978-1-312-25138-0

S&D Capital Holdings, LLC
Bristow, Virginia 20136
www.yourfinancessimplified.com

Dedication

This book is dedicated to my daughter, Olivia Brown. Daddy loves you!

Table of Contents
Part One

Part Two

Bonus Content

Preface

Disclaimer

Although the author and publisher have made every effort to ensure that the information in this book was correct at press time, the author and publisher do not assume and hereby disclaim any liability to any party for any loss, damage, or disruption caused by errors or omissions, whether such errors or omissions result from negligence, accident, or any other cause. This text is informational and intended to be a substitute for personalized advice from a professional advisor.

Your Feedback is Wanted!

As the author of this book, I'm definitely interested in hearing from you. I don't want you to buy this book, read it, and not take action. That's not cool! If you like something in the book, tell me about it! If you hate something about this book, tell me about it! How can I serve you better if I never hear what you like or dislike?

To contact me, send me an email at admin@yourfinancessimplified.com.

Why did I write this book?

I wrote this book for two reasons! First, I was tired of my friends asking me for help with their credit. I swear I would get a call just about every week from someone asking about how to improve, fix, polish, or buff their credit. It was getting way out of hand! I noticed the questions starting to get repetitive, so I decided to make a book that answers all the questions.

The second reason is I noticed that a lot of those same friends thought they needed to get professional help to fix their credit problems. Now, I have nothing against forking over money for a specialized skill or trait. For example, I would highly recommend you go to a dentist if you need a root canal, or I would highly recommend you go to a doctor if you need to have your appendix removed. However, you don't need a specialist to fix your credit! Credit professionals cannot do anything you and I can't do as it pertains to fixing credit, unlike the doctor or dentist I talked about a few sentences ago.

I'm sure you will agree that after you read this book, you will be fully equipped to fix your credit or keep your good credit. If you don't feel that way, email me and tell me about it, I can be reached at admin@yourfinancessimplified.com. Deal?

Sincerely,

Dominique Brown

Other Resources

Visit my website www.yourfinancessimplified.com for daily personal finance articles.

Credit: What Is It? Who Needs It!

I define credit as the *privilege* to borrow money and repay it at a future date. You repay the money in full or in installments. Credit may, or may not, involve the payment of interest. Say you left your wallet at home and borrow $10 from a coworker so you can eat lunch. Naturally, you promise to pay him back the next day. You have used *credit*. It is not likely that you will pay any interest on such a transaction, but you *will* return the favor.

Who Needs Credit?

Honestly, everyone needs credit, maybe not today, maybe not next week, but you will need it. Take a second to imagine life without credit. You tell me. How long would it take you to save for a new home, a new car, or even a new TV? The impact on your life would be enormous. The fact is we all need credit. Credit is the engine of capitalism. If you have any doubts about that, just examine what happened to the U.S. economy in the wake of the sub-prime mortgage crisis. The massive number of defaulted mortgage loans coupled with those anticipated to default forced banks to increase loss reserves. This significantly reduced the amount of money available for loans. Credit dried up, business growth slowed to a crawl, many businesses failed, unemployment rose, and markets crashed.

The Five Cs

Qualifying for a "lunch money" loan from a coworker is a far simpler proposition than getting an auto loan from your friendly neighborhood bank. That said many of the same tests are at play. Today, the approval or rejection of your loan request has its basis in the Fair-Isaac credit score. This modern lending tool has its foundations in the five "Cs" of credit. These so-called five "Cs" (Character, Capacity, Capital, Collateral, and Conditions) were the tools of the lending officer long before these concepts were converted to fancy algorithms and statistical outcomes. They are as valid today as they were 40 years ago, and you may benefit from a more thorough understanding of what these are and what they mean in terms of your ability to obtain credit.

1. Character

This is an important element in determining if you will get credit, whether the amount of credit received is small or large and whether you need to put up collateral or not. Character refers to the borrower's willingness and determination to pay. Back in the day, assessing the character of the borrower came from the lender's personal knowledge of the borrower's reputation in the community. However, things have changed and the lender rarely even knows the applicant and may live on the opposite side of the globe. Today, the lender relies on the credit history of the applicant as a window into the borrower's character.

2. Capacity

No matter how impeccable the character of the borrower may be, the capacity to pay is one of the most important factors. Capacity is the borrower's income relative to existing debt or credit obligations. Simply put, does the borrower have enough income to repay existing debt and the new debt?

3. Capital

We have all heard the old joke about having to prove to the banker that you don't need a loan before you can get one. That's not so far from the truth. Borrowers with assets, like a home, or equity in a home, give banker's that warm, fuzzy feeling that is absent in the case of borrowers who have no tangible net worth.

4. Collateral

This is very basic. Collateral is something of value a borrower pledges to a creditor to ensure repayment of the loan. The most straightforward example is the auto loan. The borrower purchases the car and pledges it as collateral. If the borrower defaults, the car goes back to the creditor.

5. Conditions

This one gets a bit more complicated. It is the most subjective of the five "Cs." It is the "big picture." The creditor has looked at your credit history, your income, your net worth, and your collateral. Conditions is a broader view, and it assesses the interplay of all these factors as they relate to the economy, the future outlook for your employer's business or yours, the basis of your net worth, and the value of your collateral over time. However, for consumers like you and me, conditions could be as simple as the interest rate and amount of principal. Those two things could influence the lender's desire to provide you a loan or financing.

Now that you understand the five "C's" of credit, I want to help you gain some insight into how they tie into credit scoring.

Credit Scores: Your Credit IQ

I'm pretty sure you know what a credit score is and have heard the term "credit score." Please, tell me I'm right. Well, there are good credit scores, average credit scores, great credit scores, and bad credit scores. As we just discussed, and as you probably already know, your credit score determines your ability to obtain a loan whether that loan is for a car, a mortgage, or a credit card. You being the genius you are probably even known that your credit score is a three-digit number. However, unlike natural talents, if you believe in such things, we aren't born with a credit score. We didn't take a test to get it, and we didn't wake up with it. So, where did it come from, and what is a credit score?

A Little History

Let's talk about where the credit score comes from for a minute. I'm sure you have heard of the FICO score. Well, if you haven't, Fair, Isaac and Company created the FICO score, and this company was founded in 1956 for the sole purpose of providing analytical and decision-making services to the financial community. They figured they could become ridiculously rich by creating a mythical number to determine all our fates, and two years after the company was founded, the credit scoring system was created. However, it took them 24 years of marketing and schmoozing in order to be accepted by the banks and other credit providers. I think the schmoozing and brown nosing worked, since now the FICO score is the standard for all lenders when evaluating people's credit risk.

What Makes Up a Credit Score?

The credit score is a complex mathematical formula that assigns numerical values to specific aspects of an individual's credit history. The formula, for lack of a better word, assigns values to payment history, credit balances, length of credit history, new credit inquiries, and types of credit (e.g., credit cards, auto loans, mortgages). Credit scores from www.myfico.com range in numerical value from 300 to 850 and unlike golf, the higher the score, the better!

You may be interested to know that the average credit score in the United States is 692 while the median score is 750. Here's how the credit score ties in to the five Cs we talked about earlier. The credit score reveals the **character** of the borrower and it is indicative, but to a much lesser extent, of the borrower's **capacity** to pay. What the credit score does not address is capital, collateral, conditions, or the full capacity of the borrower.

The Good News

While virtually all lenders use the FICO score when evaluating their borrowers, the good news is that credit score is not the only factor considered in making the decision to give you credit. Do you know why? Because other important factors, such as length of employment, residence, and income, also play a significant role. Remember, I explained that a credit score only partially addresses the capacity of the borrower and does not address capital, collateral, or conditions at all! In short, do not despair if you have a lower than average credit score. Other factors can offset this. One additional piece of good news is that credit scores aren't static. You *can* improve your credit score.

A Good Credit Score is an Intangible Asset

You need a good credit score because it is a valuable asset. Your credit score mirrors the risk you represent to a lender. The higher your credit score, the lower your perceived risk to the lender. Interest rates are a function of risk. It follows that a high credit score means a lower interest rate on your loan and therein lays that intangible asset we alluded to earlier. The interest savings even a 1% rate decrease makes is staggering. A $200,000.00 thirty-year mortgage at 7% has a payment of $1330.60, while at 6% the payment drops to $1199.10, a savings of $131.50 per month. That is $47,340 in savings over the life of the mortgage!

How Can I Check my Credit Score?

Now you are probably wondering, "How can I check *my* credit score?" It is easier than you might believe. By law, you are entitled to receive a copy of your credit report from each of the three credit reporting agencies (TransUnion, Experian, and Equifax) once a year. Later, we will go into some detail on ways you can do this. We will also discuss some practical ways you can improve your credit score. Now, we will take some time to learn about the different types of credit.

Credit: The Good, the Bad and the Ugly

Credit is a wonderful thing. It can make your dreams come true or turn those dreams into your worst nightmare. It is best to use credit, like all good things, in moderation and with a plan!

Managing Your Credit

Once you have succeeded in establishing some credit, think of it as a foundation on which to build a solid credit history. Your first experience with credit is likely to be "small potatoes." It might be an account with a department store, a jewelry store, or a local business. Regardless of the amount or the interest rate, which is probably steep, you must take a solemn and sober approach to repaying the debt according to the terms agreed upon. Do not be late with payments! Make sure you pay far enough in advance of the due date for the payment to reach your creditor on time and never pay less than you agreed to pay (it is okay to pay more). We will have more on this later.

Types of Credit

When it comes to credit, there are just two types of credit and two sub types of credit you should be concerned with—installment credit and revolving credit.

Installment Credit

Installment credit, which is sometimes called closed-end, is a loan in which the borrower receives the total proceeds of the loan up front and repays in equal periodic payments, usually monthly, on a specified date and for a specific number of periods. The loan's structure is such that *on-time* payments reduce the loan to a zero balance at maturity.

An excellent example of installment credit is the auto loan. Repayment is in the form of equal payments, every month, for a specified number of monthly payments, which result in a defined end (maturity) date. Now, you should know that there are variations on this, no doubt dreamed up by bored bankers on those inclement days when they were unable to escape to the relative excitement of the country club's golf course. For example, there are balloon payments, pick up payments, variable rate, interest only, and several other exotics that you will not likely encounter in your lifetime. Just know they exist and have the good sense to avoid them.

Revolving Credit

Revolving credit, also known as open-ended credit, differs significantly from installment credit.

First, you do not receive any loan proceeds when you sign the loan agreement. Payments are neither fixed nor equal. Instead, payments are a function of the outstanding loan balance at the end of thirty-day intervals. The only similarity is that you make payments on a monthly basis.

Your credit card is the best example of this credit type, but there are certainly other versions, such as a home equity *line of credit.* Revolving credit is *the most* dangerous type of credit to own. The language of revolving credit contracts has more twists and turns than an episode of "World's Deadliest Roads." However, the Credit Card Accountability Responsibility and Disclosure Act of 2009 (wow, what a name), or the Credit Card Act of 2009 for short, changed a lot of the sneaky stuff. Basically, the Credit Card Act of 2009 provided comprehensive credit card reform for the benefit of the consumer, by requiring that things are written in plain English. Just to be safe, when you hear, "revolving credit" think "revolver" and put yourself on guard. We will have more on this later.

Secured

This is a form of installment or revolving credit that is tied to a lien on an asset you own. A great example of a secured installment loan is your car loan. Your car loan is tied to your car, so if you stop paying your monthly car payment, the lender will repossess the car. Get it? The same is true with your home. Your mortgage is considered to be a secured installment loan. Meaning, the loan, which is also known as your mortgage, is backed by your house. If you fail to pay your mortgage you will be foreclosed.

Unsecured

When your credit is unsecured, you simply give your word to the creditor that you will repay what you borrow. Credit card, medical, and utilities bills are all examples of unsecured credit.

The Good, Bad and Ugly

While I view all credit as a tool to accomplish a particular goal or task, much like a hammer or gun, I use all of the types of credit mentioned above for various reasons and do not think any particular type of credit is bad. Now, some people get into trouble with revolving credit, also known as credit cards, but that doesn't mean the type of credit in itself is bad. It's just like the phrase, "Guns don't kill people. People kill people." Credit cards don't make you spend money. It's your spending habits that make you spend money. Credit cards, like guns, just make completing the mission easier.

Now that you know a little bit about credit scores and the different types of credit, we'll take a look at how your actions affect your credit score.

Taking Charge of Your Credit Score

Credit scores don't just happen. Good or bad, you earn it by *your* actions. Accepting this fact is the first step in controlling your credit destiny. As I said earlier, your credit score is just one component in the decision to approve or deny your loan request. However, it is of *huge* importance. Think of the credit score as the maître d' of the credit banquet. If you don't make the cut in terms of credit score, you aren't going to get a table, and no one will see anything of your other, possibly offsetting, positive qualities. Each lender establishes cut-off points unique to its business model. It may be difficult to get your head around, but the fact is, many of your hopes, dreams, and aspirations hinge on this three-digit number.

Your Credit Score

The three major credit-reporting agencies are Experian, TransUnion, and Equifax. Each one will generate a different credit score for you. The reason is not all creditors report to all three credit-reporting agencies. They may report to only one or two. The result, obviously, is that disparate information means different credit scores. Many companies offer to provide your credit score— some for a fee while others claim to do it free. Regardless of how you obtain it, the score you receive will not be the score your lender sees. In my view, it is *more important* to know what is in your credit report. It is, after all, this information that is the basis of the score's calculation. Knowing the information the credit-reporting agency has in your file and that the information is accurate gives you the best opportunity to improve your score.

The Basis of Your FICO Score

I say it is more important to know what is in your credit report than to know your actual score. This is true because the algorithm FICO uses to calculate your score uses the information in that report, and this is that information.

- Payment information on your accounts
- Public record and collection items
- Details on late or missed payments and public record and collection items
- How many accounts show no late payments
- The amount owed on all accounts
- The amount owed on all accounts and on different types of accounts
- How many accounts have balances
- How much of the total credit line is being used on credit cards and other revolving credit accounts
- How much of an installment loan is still owed compared to the original loan amount
- How long your credit accounts have been established in general
- How long specific credit accounts have been established
- How long it has been since you used certain accounts
- How many new accounts you have
- How long it has been since you opened a new account
- How many recent requests for credit you have made as indicated by inquires to the credit reporting agencies
- The length of time since the credit report inquiries were made by lenders
- Whether you have a good recent credit history, following past payment problems
- What kinds of credit accounts you have
- The total number accounts you have

The list I mentioned above gets rolled up into the following five categories:

1. Payment History
2. Amounts Owed
3. Length of Credit History
4. New Credit
5. Types of New Credit

Your Fico score is based on the five categories mentioned above. However, the weight of each category is not the same because some things are more important than others. Here is how the five categories break down in terms of importance and weight.

1. Payment History – 35%
2. Amounts Owed – 30%
3. Length of Credit History – 15%
4. New Credit – 10%
5. Types of Credit Used – 10%

Knowledge is Power

All right we now know what elements of the credit report the FICO score is based upon. Armed with that information, we can determine what we should guard against. Clearly, the number of accounts you have had is a factor, and so is how many times and to what degree these accounts have been past due. FICO also seems to be interested in the number of times you have applied for credit and how many open accounts (specifically credit cards and installment loans) you have. FICO is also keen on your total available revolving credit and the total amount of credit you are using. They are looking at maxed out credit cards, and they are focusing on recent bankruptcy filings, tax liens, and judgments. Lastly, they appear interested in your most recently opened account.

It Isn't Rocket Science

It is clear from this information what you need to pay attention to the terms of your credit. Factors such as over or under use of credit, paying late, making too many attempts to open accounts, the number of obligations you have, credit card limits, balances, and negatives like judgments and tax liens are all in play when it comes to your credit score. The result of FICO's mathematical wizardry is a score ranging from 350 to 850. Scores from 350 to 639 represent borrowers that are high risk. Scores from 640 to 719 represent a medium risk, and scores from 720 to 850 represent a low risk to lenders.

Now that you know what affects your credit score, I'll tell you how to improve it.

Achieving Your Goals

In the next several paragraphs, I am going to go into more detail than you may care to read on the points you need to focus on to improve your credit score. Achieving your goals and aspirations may rest on your ability to obtain the credit you need at the lowest possible interest rate.

Into the Weeds

I want to take you through each item that is significant to your credit score. A thorough understanding of these is the first step in taking control of your credit destiny.

- Payment Information on Many Types of Accounts - These include credit cards, retail accounts like department store cards, installment loans, finance company accounts, and mortgage loans. Basically, anything that can be found in your credit report will be tracked for timely payments.

- Public Record and Collection Items - These are things like bankruptcies, foreclosures, suits, wage attachments, liens, and judgments. Quite frankly, these are very serious. You want to avoid these like the plague! However, older items and items with small amounts will count less than more recent items with larger amounts. Bankruptcies will stay on your credit report for 7-10 years, depending on the type.

- Details on Late or Missed Payments and Public Record and Collection Items - Your FICO score will take into consideration how late your payments were, the recency of the late payment, and how much of a late payment. Obviously the later the payment, the greater the impact it will have on your score. A 60-day late payment is not as significant as a 120-day late payment, but keep in mind recency and frequency count as well. A 60-day late payment made just one month ago will hurt your score more than a 120 day late payment made three or four years ago.

- How Many Accounts Show no Late Payments - This one is self-explanatory. Having accounts with no late payments will definitely improve your score.

- The Amount Owed on All Accounts - This is a simple calculation of how much you owe on your accounts. Keep in mind that even if you pay off your credit cards in full, a term we call Pay in Full or PIF, your credit report will show a balance on those cards. The total balance on your last statement is what shows up in your credit report.

- The Amount Owed on All Accounts and on Different Types of Accounts - This one takes into account the total amount owed on all your accounts and the amount you owe on specific types of accounts, such as credit cards and installment loans.

- Whether You Are Showing a Balance on Certain Types of Accounts - Having a very small balance compared to total available credit without missing a payment shows that you have managed your credit responsibly. However, closing accounts that are in good standing will not raise your credit score at all. This credit metric dispels the myth of "you should close your credit cards to improve your score."

- How Many Accounts Have Balances – This one is also self-explanatory, but it means that you shouldn't have 10 accounts where all 10 have balances. You want to keep in mind that a large number can indicate higher risk to a lender.

- How Much of the Total Credit Line is Being Used on Credit Cards and Other Types of Revolving Credit - This is also known as your credit utilization. People who are close to maxing out their credit cards are a greater risk, and this high credit utilization may signal that they'll have trouble making payments in the future.

- How Much of an Installment Loan is Still Owed Compared to the Original Loan Amounts - If you borrowed $20,000 for a boat and paid back $4,000, you owe (with interest) more than 80% of the original loan. To FICO paying down installment loans is a good sign that you are able and willing to manage and repay debt.

- How Long Your Credit Accounts Have Been Established - This is the average number of years you've had credit. This is the age of your oldest account, the age of your newest account, and an average of all your accounts. You should never ever get credit just to get it!

- How Long Specific Credit Accounts Have Been Established - This is a part of calculating your average credit history length, and it is a look at each account and when it was established.

- How Long It Has Been Since You Used a Certain Account – This is a look at each account to determine if it's active or inactive.

- How Many Accounts You Have - This is a look at how many new accounts you have and the type of each account. For example, how many new credit cards (revolving credit).

- How Many Recent Requests for Credit that You Have Made as Indicated by Inquiries to the Credit Reporting Agencies - How frequently you shop for credit could hurt your score! Inquiries remain on your credit report for two years, but your FICO score only looks at the last 12 months of inquires.

- The Length of Time since the Credit Report Inquires Were Made by Lenders – This is not much different from the explanation above. My tip, don't keep applying for credit just because you have a pulse. Only shop for and accept credit when you need it.

- Whether You Have a Good Recent Credit History Following Past Payment Problems - You can raise your score by re-establishing credit and making payments on time after a period of late payments. See, there is hope after all!

- What Kind of Credit Accounts You Have - This is where it looks for a good healthy mix of credit—a nice balance of revolving credit and installment credit. It's looking for your experience with the different types of credit that we discussed earlier.

- How Many of Each - Your FICO score looks at the total number of accounts you have and too many isn't necessarily a problem. It depends on your particular credit profile.

What's Hot and What's Not

We've learned how your FICO score is based on the information in your credit report, past and present. In this section, we will discuss the varying degrees of importance the FICO algorithm places on that information. Think of it as a beauty contest. Thirty percent for talent, twenty-five percent for swimsuit, twenty-five percent for evening gown, and twenty percent for the stupid question. Yes, FICO is a lot like that!

Credit is a Beautiful Thing

Earlier I mentioned the proprietary nature of the FICO formula. Like the formula for Coca-Cola, Colonel Sander's secret recipe, or the recipe for Bush's Baked Beans, the formula for calculating the FICO score is closely held. We do know, with some degree of certainty, the judging rules. Proper implementation of the knowledge provided here and in the previous chapter can result in a truly beautiful credit score.

Payment History

We have already had the discussion on payment history. To reiterate, there are dire consequences for not paying on time. Being late is one of the worst things you can be in life; it's also one of the worst things for your credit score. Now I'll tell you where the rubber meets the road. Fair, Isaac and Company, esteemed developer of the credit scoring system, places **35%** of its emphasis on your payment history. Now you understand why *I* placed so much emphasis on this earlier.

Amounts Owed

A full **30%** of your score revolves (no pun intended) around the relationship between your credit card limits and your credit card balances. In the trade they call this *credit utilization,* and it measures the ratio between your credit limits and the balances owed. For example, if you have a credit card with a $10,000 limit and your balance owed is $7200, your credit utilization ratio is 72%. If you total all your credit limits and all your balances owed (balances, not payments), you can easily calculate your overall credit utilization ratio. The effect on your credit score is inversely proportional to the utilization ratio. In short, the higher the percentage the lower your credit score, got it? The consensus is that your utilization rate should be in the 20% range.

Length of Credit History

It is said, "The best predictor of future behavior is past behavior." Nothing rings truer when it comes to your credit score. Of course, the longer the history of behavior, in our case, payment history, the more accurately the future behavior can be predicted. It is for this reason that the length of your credit history makes up **15%** of your FICO score.

New Credit

I caution you now! Do not assume a cavalier attitude with regard to applying for unneeded, unnecessary, or superfluous credit. It represents a danger to your credit score on so many levels. The FICO folks agree and, as a result, **10%** of your credit score is tied to new accounts and inquiries, which, as you now know, are generated every time you attempt to open an account. Changing your habits now can make a real difference in this category. The reason is they do not consider inquiries that are more than one year old. As a result, stopping the practice now will quickly reap rewards. In this category, you are presented with a rare opportunity to make an improvement by doing ***nothing***!

Types of Credit in Use

The variety or *mix* of account types that are included in your credit report defines the remaining **10%** of your credit score. You may recall that I introduced you earlier to the two main types of credit and the two sub types of credit. By way of a reminder, they are installment, revolving, secured, and unsecured. A mix of these types demonstrates your ability and reveals your experience in properly managing different types of credit. Given the small impact on your credit score, I strongly discourage you from opening new accounts for the sole purpose of increasing the variety of credit you have on file. This could well be offset by the impact resulting from inquiries, and in the case of revolving credit (credit cards), there is the additional risk of an adverse impact on your credit utilization ratio.

Now, you can keep reading to learn about all of the things that *don't* affect your credit score.

A Study in Objectivity

Regardless of your personal feelings on credit scoring, one thing stands out as a positive for everyone involved in the process—objectivity.

The Credit Cathedral

Many of you reading this are too young to recall the heady days when bankers operated on the 3-6-3 rule. This simplistic, but possibly all too accurate jibe, suggests that bankers paid depositors 3 percent, lent the money at 6 percent, and hit the golf course by 3 PM. In those days, banks built main branches to rival cathedrals, and no one would think of stopping in to apply for a loan dressed in anything less than his Sunday best.

Modern Lending

Well, those days are certainly gone and really, the only thing I miss is that 3 percent return on deposits. These days, you rarely come face to face with a decision maker on a visit to your local bank. Bankers and other lenders handle credit applications and decisions to approve or decline them electronically, with the aid of that FICO score we have spent so much time together dissecting. The reality is that this is a positive for the vast majority of the borrowing public.

Conspicuously Absent

Using the credit score as the principal criteria to consider a loan request removes virtually all subjective influences from the decision making process. Consider for a moment the litany of factors the FICO methodology does not consider:

- Ethnicity
- Religion
- National Origin
- Age (provided the applicant has the capacity to contract)
- Gender
- Marital Status
- Sexual Orientation

What this means is that even if you are a 75-year-old, divorced, Burmese, Hmong man, who is a pre-op transgender, animist attracted to men and your FICO score is 720, you have the same odds for loan approval as anyone else with a similar credit score and similar credit request.

Consumer Credit Protection Act

In addition to the objective and equitable approach provided borrowers by the FICO score, the Consumer Credit Protection Act expands borrowers' rights even further under Title VII, Equal Credit Opportunity in Section 701. This federal law prohibits any creditor to discriminate against any applicant with respect to any aspect of a credit transaction based on race, color, religion, national origin, sex, marital status, or age (provided the applicant has the capacity to contract). Under this law, a creditor cannot discriminate against applicants that receive public assistance. Neither can they hold it against you if you have exercised any of your rights under the Consumer Credit Protection Act.

The language in the law that permits the use of credit scoring is as follows: "It shall not constitute discrimination for purposes of this title for a creditor to *use any empirically derived credit system* which considers age if such system is demonstrably and statistically sound in accordance with regulations of the Bureau of Consumer Financial Protection."

So, credit approval is left up to computers?

Not entirely! Most creditors use the credit score to eliminate applicants that do not warrant further consideration. Applicants who make that cut must still clear the hurdles established in the remaining four of the five Cs of credit we talked about earlier. Think of your good credit score as a tool used to win the first heat. You still have the real race to run. Credit scores, if you recall, only address the first C of credit, the remaining four Cs require human intervention. That is why I felt that it was necessary to explain the five Cs to you, the reader.

Want to Find Your Credit Score?

Of course you do, but as I have told you, you are never likely to get the score your lender has for you. Each credit-reporting agency will offer a credit score for you, and no two are the same. In my view, you don't need your credit score. Does knowing your IQ make you any more intelligent? You are better off knowing what is *in your credit report*. Armed with this information, you can develop a strategy based on what you have learned here to improve your credit score no matter what that three-digit number may be. If you stubbornly insist on having your credit score, I will help you with that in the next section.

A Good Credit Score: What's in It for You?

Society is becoming increasingly dependent on using credit to make purchases and decisions. These days, good credit is used for more than just getting a credit card or a loan. Your credit score is a resource, a virtual guarantee, which allows you to acquire funds, assets, and necessities, insurance, and even a job. More and more businesses are making the case that you must have good credit before they extend products or services to you. Your credit score could be a gateway to financial freedom and freedom from financial stress.

I promised you earlier that I would provide information on getting your credit reports and you will find that here.

Online - Go to www.annualcreditreport.com - this is the only *legitimate* source for access to your *free* annual credit report.

By Phone - Call (877) 322-8228. This is the best choice for those who are not Internet-savvy or have no access to the Internet.

By Mail - Mail a request to Annual Credit Report Request Service, P.O. Box 105281, Atlanta, GA, 30348-5281

PLEASE NOTE: The information provided above directs your inquiries to a centralized agency, established and supported by all three credit-reporting agencies in order to comply with the 2003 Fair and Accurate Credit Transactions Act. You are entitled to one free report, annually, from each agency. If you go to any other source, including the reporting agencies themselves, you may incur charges for your report(s).

If you want your credit score, there are multiple Internet sources, most you will have to pay for, some you can get "free" by subscription, but if you forget to cancel, you're on the hook for a monthly fee. I have maintained throughout, that an actual credit score is not something you really need to know. Knowing how it works coupled with the knowledge of what is on your credit report is, in my view, enough information. That being said, I have no doubt you will follow your own path.

I hope you have found this information thought provoking, useful, and easily understood. It is sufficiently comprehensive to meet the needs of the average consumer. I hope I leave you with the notion that good credit has value. Protect it, guard it, and respect it for what it is—your most valuable, intangible resource.

Part Two

How to Heal Your Bad Credit

Ridding yourself of bad credit is a lot like removing that stupid tattoo you got in high school. You have outgrown it, divorced it, or lost a job over it; therefore, it has to go! Tattoo removal is a process to be sure. It may take several laser treatments, over a period of weeks, months, or perhaps longer to completely remove the ink. Cleaning up your credit history is like that too but without the laser!

No Quick Fix

It took more than a day or two to earn that poor credit history, so please, don't expect that you can fix it overnight because you cannot. No matter how many hyped-up claims you have read on the back of matchbooks, in the personals of sleazy newspapers, or from infomercials and ads on the web, this is not a quick process.

Credit is a multi-billion dollar business. While there are over 400 credit bureaus scattered across the world, most are owned by or affiliated with one of the "big three," which include Experian PLC, Equifax, Inc., and TransUnion Corporation. In 2010, Experian had gross revenues of $3.88 billion, and Equifax had gross revenues of $1.86 billion, and TransUnion Corporation, which is privately held, had gross revenues of $1.02 billion. Additionally, I can tell you that in February 2012 the private equity firm, Advent International, agreed to buy TransUnion Corporation for the tidy sum of $3 billion.

The points I want to make are these:

- Credit-reporting agencies are powerful
- Credit-reporting agencies have tremendous financial resources
- Credit-reporting agencies wouldn't be powerful and rich if they weren't smart

I make these points so you will believe me when I tell you that the majority of the claims made by credit repair companies are patently false. Do you really think some upstart little company, run by a fast-talking man in a polyester suit and clip-on tie is capable of manipulating billion dollar companies? Trust me when I tell you, they can't do anything that you can't do yourself. That's why I wrote this book, I was tired of people overpaying for simple advice. Instead of spending money and going with a company to clean up your credit, save your money and put it toward your bills. That said if you are ready to get on the path to repairing your credit, read on.

Knowledge is Power

You may think your credit score is low, you probably know why your credit score is messed up, but without seeing your credit report, how can you know the full story? Without a credit report in your hands you cannot possibly develop a strategy to heal (I prefer "heal" rather than "repair" your credit score.

The first step in healing your credit is to get your credit report.

Order Your Credit Report

Getting a credit report is easy! When I say easy, you're going to be pissed after I tell you how easy it is. Not only is it easy, you even have a legal right to get one free credit report from all 400 of the credit bureaus each year. However, you don't have to get all 400—that would be crazy. You only need to get one credit report from the big three (Equifax, Transunion, Experian).

Make sure you stagger when you order your free credit reports. What I mean by this is that you should get one free credit report every four months. For example, in January order your Equifax credit report. In May order your Transunion credit report, and in September order your Experian credit report. This will get you all year coverage.

The methods I'm going to show you below are the only legitimate ways to order a free credit report. By legitimate, I mean it's specified in law that this is where you go to order a free credit report.

Ordering Your Credit Report via the Internet

The best way to get your credit report is online. If you do not have a computer or internet access at home, you can stop by your local public library (free) or drop by an Internet cafe. It really is the best and quickest way to accomplish this task.

Step 1: Go to www.annualcreditreport.com.

Step 2: In the upper left hand corner of the home page, you will see "START HERE." From the drop down box, select the name of the state where you live and then click on "Request Report.

Step 3: This brings you to a screen that asks your first name, middle initial, last name, and suffix, which you choose from a drop down list. Then you must enter your date of birth. You select the month and the day from a drop down list, and you type in the four digit year. Next, you must enter your social security number. You must provide all nine digits, but you can opt to have only the last four digits appear on your report for printing or viewing purposes.

It is not a bad idea to select this option. It keeps your full social security number confidential. After that, enter your current/recent address. If you have not been at your current address for at least two years, the site asks for your previous address. Click on the appropriate "yes" or "no" button and enter your previous address if your answer is "no." To confirm that you are human, you re-enter the characters seen in the colorful "captcha" box and click "submit." Finally, click the blue "continue" button.

PLEASE PROVIDE ALL OF THE PERSONAL INFORMATION REQUIRED BELOW.

This information is needed to begin the process of determining your identity and finding your credit report. Please refer to our Privacy Policy and Security and Encryption Policy to learn more about the use of and protection of this information.

Norton SECURED
powered by VeriSign

* = Required Field

---

*First Name: [   ]   Middle Initial: [   ]   *Last Name: [   ]   Suffix: [▼]

*Date of Birth: [▼] [▼] [   ]
Month   Day   Year (YYYY)

*Social Security Number: [   ] - [ ] - [   ]
SSN will be encrypted for your protection

☐ Check this box if, for security reasons, you want no more than the last four digits of your Social Security Number to appear when you view or print your credit report.

Current Address
*Line 1: [   ]   Line 2: [   ]
*City: [   ]   *State: [Virginia ▼]   *Zip Code: [   ]

Have you lived at your current address for at least 2 years?

◉ Yes
○ No (If 'No', please provide previous address)

Previous Address
Line 1: [   ]   Line 2: [   ]
City: [   ]   State: [▼]   Zip Code: [   ]

For added security please type in the characters you see in the picture on the left, in the box below.

V1 3SFVIF   *Enter Characters: [   ]

If you are unable to see the characters, please go to the alternate request page . Learn more about this security feature.

[CONTINUE]

Step 4: This brings you to a page at which you select one or more of the three nationwide consumer credit-reporting companies from which you may request your free credit report. In another section of the book I'm going to walk you through a few sections of my free Equifax report, so if you want to follow along (and I suggest you should) you should order the Equifax report. Get it? Got it? Good!

I recommend you choose one at a time. So, make your choice, click "next," and you will be transferred to that company's site. The next screen asks additional questions to verify your identity. These vary by company. Answer the question(s) and click submit. Don't be surprised if you see some off the wall questions that don't pertain to you, just choose the appropriate response. Following the instructions, print your credit report. Then return to the Annual Credit Report website if you wish to retrieve your credit report from a different reporting agency. That is all there is to it!

When you visit the credit bureau's website, no matter if it is Equifax, Transunion or Experian, you will be solicited to buy your credit score. At this point in the game, you do not need your credit score. Also, the credit score that they provide is not your official credit score. The only official credit score is the one you get from www.myfico.com. However, the three credit bureaus will offer you a credit score based on some algorithm they made up to satisfy the itch of needing to see your credit score with the free credit report. I don't blame them—never let a potential customer go to waste! However, I urge you *not* to spend your money on the score just yet.

Ordering Your Credit Report by Phone

If you don't have internet access, access to a library, or a friend who has Internet access, I added the procedure to order your credit report by phone.

Step 1: Call 1 (877) 322-8228.

Step 2: Follow the automated instructions.

Your reports will be mailed to you within 15 days. Please, allow 2-3 weeks for delivery.

Order Your Credit Report by Mail

I personally wouldn't order my credit report via mail, but I'm adding the third method here anyway. Why wouldn't I order my credit report via mail? Well, you have to go online and download a request form, print the form, and mail it to the company. Why go through all that hassle? If you're online already just use the online method and get your credit report immediately.

However, for those who like to burn trees.

Step 1: Print the request form by going to:
http://www.ftc.gov/bcp/edu/resources/forms/requestformfinal.pdf

Step 2: Print and complete the form

Step 3: Mail the form to:

Annual Credit Report Request Service
P.O. Box 105281

Your reports will be mailed to you within 15 days. Please, allow 2-3 weeks for delivery.

Seriously, though, do yourself a favor and order via the Internet, so you don't have to wait three weeks to finish this book.

PLEASE NOTE: The information provided above directs your inquiries to a centralized agency, established and supported by all three credit-reporting agencies in compliance with the 2003 Fair and Accurate Credit Transactions Act. You are entitled to <u>one</u> free report, annually from <u>each</u> agency. If you go to any other source, including the reporting agencies themselves, you may incur charges for your report(s).

I Have My Credit Report—Now What?

Familiarize yourself with the report. Read it over. Read it over again. You may be overwhelmed at first, but I'll walk you through it. Think of it this way, you didn't immediately know how to ride a bike did you? Don't lie! You had on training wheels to guide you. This part of the book is the training wheels for going through your credit report. It will all make sense, I promise. Now let's get started.

All credit reports have the same basic types of information:

- An ID number or Confirmation Number
- Identifying data (your personal information)
  - Name (including any nicknames or variations)
  - Home addresses (past and present)
  - Date of birth
  - Spouse's name (if applicable)
  - Past and present employers
  - Social Security number
- Credit history
- Inquiries
- Public record information
  - Judgments
  - Tax liens
  - Bankruptcies
  - Convictions

Each agency uses a different format, but all contain the above five elements. Now, let's walk through your Equifax report. Get your highlighter out!

Checking my Credit Report for Errors

I suggest you print the credit report out when following these steps. However, if you want to be fancy, you can use the highlighter feature in your PDF viewing software. I'm all about saving trees—this is why we didn't order via mail right?

With credit report and highlighter in hand, let's review the Equifax credit report. The first thing you want to check is your name. If your name is not spelled right, highlight it. Next, highlight the confirmation number. You're going to need the confirmation number for disputing inaccuracies in your credit report.

Next you should see the table of contents. Your Equifax credit report will be broken down into nine sections. Each section is very important!

Section Title	Section Description
1. Credit Summary	Summary of account activity
2. Account Information	Detailed account information
3. Inquiries	Companies that have requested or viewed your credit information
4. Negative Information	Bankruptcies, liens, garnishments and other judgments
5. Personal Information	Personal data, addresses, employment history
6. Dispute File Information	How to dispute information found on this credit report
7. Summary of Your Rights Under the FCRA	Summary of Your Rights Under the FCRA
8. Remedying the Effects of Identity Theft	Remedying the Effects of Identity Theft
9. Your Rights Under State Law	Your Rights Under State Law

Following that is your Credit Summary, which gives you a quick snapshot your credit report. In this section you will see the following:

Accounts

- Type of open accounts
- Number of open accounts per type
- Total number of open accounts
- Balances owed per type
- Total balance owed
- Available credit per type
- Total available credit
- Credit limit per type
- Total credit limit
- Debt to credit ratio
- Monthly payment amount per type
- Total monthly payment amount
- Accounts carrying a balance per type

- Total accounts carrying a balance

On your credit report you may see something that says other. You may be wondering, "What the heck is Other?" Other simply means that those are accounts that do not fall into other categories, like 30 day accounts such as Amex Charge cards.

Account Age - length of credit history

Inquiries - Requests for your Credit History - inquiries in the last two years

Potentially Negative Information

- Public records
- Negative accounts
- Collections

Check all of these to ensure they make sense. If you have anything under "potentially negative information," double and triple check it.

Now that the Summary is out the way, let's look at one of your accounts. This is what entries will look like:

Account Number:	430679160344XXXX	Current Status:	PAYS AS AGREED
Account Owner:	Individual Account.	High Credit:	$ 29,219
Type of Account :	Revolving	Credit Limit:	$ 50,000
Term Duration:		Terms Frequency:	Monthly (due every month)
Date Opened:	10/30/2008	Balance:	$ 0
Date Reported:	11/12/2012	Amount Past Due:	
Date of Last Payment:	12/2011	Actual Payment Amount:	
Scheduled Payment Amount:		Date of Last Activity:	12/2011
Date Major Delinquency First Reported:		Months Reviewed:	45
Creditor Classification:		Activity Description:	N/A
Charge Off Amount:		Deferred Payment Start Date:	
Balloon Payment Amount:		Balloon Payment Date:	
Date Closed:		Type of Loan:	Credit Card
Date of First Delinquency:	N/A		
Comments:			

Look in these areas for errors

Account Number	Look for incorrect numbers
Account Owner	Make sure the ownership of the account is correct. For example, if this is a joint account instead of an individual account, highlight it.
Type of Account	Make sure the type of account is correct. For example, if you know this is an installment account or mortgage rather than a revolving account, highlight it.
Term Duration	Not all accounts will have a duration. However, Installment accounts and Mortgages should show a duration. Make sure your auto loans, mortgages, and home equity lines have the correct duration. For example, they will show something like 30 years or 72 months.
Date Opened	Make sure the correct date is here. For example, if the account was opened in 2001 instead of 2008, you want to fix that.
Scheduled Payment Amount	When dealing with installment or mortgages this section is usually filled in. For example, if you have a $200 dollar car payment, make sure it's $200 instead of $500.
Date Major Delinquency First Reported	If you are late in paying your debt, make sure they have the correct debt. Blank is good!
Charge Off Amount	If you had any debt charged off, make sure the correct amount is here.
Balloon Payment Amount	Make sure this says the correct amount, if you have a balloon payment.
Date Closed	Ensure closed account date reflects the date you actually closed the account.

Date of First Delinquency	N/A or Blank means never delinquent. However, if you see a date here, make sure the date is correct.
Credit Status	Paid As Agreed is a good thing. Anything other than that you want to make sure it's accurate.
High Credit	This is the highest balance the account has ever been. It doesn't mean much, but if even is this number is wrong you want it fixed.
Credit Limit	You want to make sure all your accounts show a credit limit. Some creditors, especially credit cards, don't report this amount, but you want this to show up on your credit report because this is how your credit utilization gets calculated. Make sure the correct credit limit is there. You can simply dispute it if it is not listed.
Balance	This one is tricky, your credit report reflects what you owe the day you are issued your statement. So, it's roughly 30 days behind. However, make sure it's saying the right stuff.
Amount Past Due	Do you owe money? If not, this is a non-issue! If you do owe money, make sure it's right.
Date of Last Activity	This is probably one of the most incorrect errors on your credit report. Now if your account is in good standing and you just paid the bill, this should be fairly recent. However, if this is a collection account and you know you haven't paid in six years, you want to make sure this reflects the right information. More on this later.

Looking through your credit report for errors wasn't so bad now was it? Don't forget to highlight it as you go! Moving on to address and other personal information, you want to review all of it to ensure that it is correct. If it's off, highlight it.

What's Not in My Credit Report?

I suspect you will be more surprised by what is not in the report than you will by what is in the report. Quite often, you will find that much of your actual credit experience is not in the report. If you have reports in hand from all three reporting agencies, you will also notice that the credit histories do not necessarily match item for item (or as they call them in the industry…"trades"). Trades are the creditors you have done business with over the years.

The reason for this disparity is simply explained. Not all creditors report to the credit bureaus. Even if they do report, they may only report to one or two. Alternatively, they may only report derogatory information. Sometimes they only report the fact that they opened an account with you and do not report on a monthly basis. As a result, your "trade" information can vary from agency to agency. The same is true with inquiries. Many creditors only pull a report from one credit-reporting agency, and therefore, the inquiry only shows up on *that* credit-reporting agency's records.

Public record information is, for lack of a better word, a crapshoot. Some agencies do a good job, catching most things most of the time, while others do not. If you find that your reports do not reflect all your transgressions, just count your blessings and shut your mouth.

No Score

Believe it or not, when you go online for your free credit report, your credit score isn't included. Why? Well, the credit report companies offer free reports in order to lure you in and get you to purchase your score, which is what loan companies look at when determining your credit worthiness.

Cash on Hand

Your free credit score will NOT include information on the amount of money you currently have in your checking and savings accounts. This information is too liquid, and it doesn't matter how much money you have on hand if you aren't paying your debt, which is all the three credit bureaus care about.

Your Debit Cards

Using your debit card or pre-paid credit card is a good way to stay out of debt, but using them won't help your credit score. Why? Debit cards and pre-paid credit cards are basically the tools used for the section above–cash on hand, and you know by now, that section isn't considered by the bureaus as report worthy.

Old Bankruptcies

If you filed for bankruptcy more than 10 years ago, this information will not be included on your current credit report. Why? After 10 years, the three credit bureaus consider this debt to be old and are willing to throw you a bone. They assume that the debts attached to the bankruptcy have been paid and that you are more credit wise because of your experiences.

Seven Year Old Debt

Your free credit report will NOT include information on charged-off accounts or collections debts that are older than seven years.

Unnecessary Personal Information

The three credit bureaus are very good about keeping track of where you've lived, the amount you've settled a debt for, and how many days late you are on paying your Children's Place Card, but they have no idea that you're originally from Ghana, that you practice Islam, or that you are a woman. Your credit report will not contain information pertaining to things outside of the realm of money (or tracking you down to get the money that you owe). You won't find information about your religion, gender, nationality, political affiliations, ethnicity, criminal records, or medical records.

How to Get Errors off my Credit Report

Now that you know what a credit report does and does not contain, you need to know how to clean it up if there are any errors. This is a very important step when it comes to healing your credit, and there are three ways to launch an investigation about information on your credit report in order to dispute incorrect information.

- Online
- Phone
- Mail

I will walk you through how to dispute information with the Equifax credit report that we just checked for errors.

Dispute Online

Step 1: For Equifax you initiate an online dispute by going to www.ai.equifax.com.

You will see a screen which gives an overview of the three step process and two buttons "Get Started" and "Check Status." Click "Get Started."

Get Started in 3 easy steps

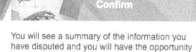

You will be able to choose what area of your current credit file to review. This will allow you to quickly identify and dispute any inaccurate information that may be reporting.

You will see a summary of the information you have disputed and you will have the opportunity to change/modify your dispute.

You are now ready to *Submit* your dispute. Simply click *Submit* and we will verify your disputed information. Once completed, you will be notified by email.

What would you like to do? Start a dispute or check your status?

In *Get Started* you will be allowed to start an investigation on items within your credit file.
In *Check Status* you will be able to view the status of previous disputes.

Get Started   **Check Status**

Step 2: You will be brought to a screen which will ask for some personal information and the confirmation number of the credit report. Grab the confirmation number from the credit report and enter it. You will have to put in your first name, last name, social security number, date of birth, current address, city, state, zip code, if you lived in your current residence for two years, and your email. Don't forget to click the button "Show only the last 4 of my SSN." Check the box to continue and hit the "Continue" button.

Let's locate your credit file

Before you can get started, we'll need to find your Equifax Credit File. To help us locate your file, you will need to provide the following information.

*Indicates a mandatory field

10-Digit Confirmation Number	[_____] What is this?
*First Name	[_____]
*Last Name	[_____]
Initial	[____] Suffix [____ ÷]
*Social Security Number	[___] - [___] - [____]
*Date of Birth	[Month ÷] / [Day ÷] / [Year]
*Current Address	[_____]
*City	[_____]
*State	[____ ÷]
*Zip Code	[_____]
Have you lived at your current address for more than 2 years?	⦿ Yes ◯ No
*Email	[_____]
*Confirmation Email	[_____]

☐ Show only last 4 digits of my SSN
* ☐ To continue, click to agree to Online Delivery of Results

Continue

25

Step 3: You will be brought to a screen to select your dispute.

You have four options to choose from:

- Personal Information
- Accounts
- Negative Information
- Inquiries

Select which option you need to dispute.

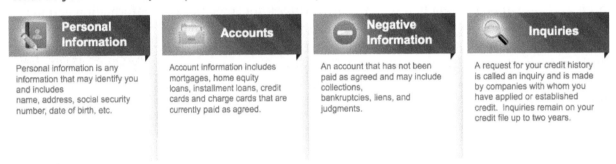

Welcome

Please select the area of your credit file you prefer to review. This is a current copy of your file and has the latest information available. Please review carefully.

What do you want to dispute? (Select a section below.)

Personal Information	Accounts	Negative Information	Inquiries
Personal information is any information that may identify you and includes name, address, social security number, date of birth, etc.	Account information includes mortgages, home equity loans, installment loans, credit cards and charge cards that are currently paid as agreed.	An account that has not been paid as agreed and may include collections, bankruptcies, liens, and judgments.	A request for your credit history is called an inquiry and is made by companies with whom you have applied or established credit. Inquiries remain on your credit file up to two years.

Step 4: Once you click the area you want to fix, you will be brought to the applicable section. Let's say you click personal information. You will be brought to a screen which shows your name, social security number, birth date, address information, other names, employment history, alerts, and consumer statements.

As of Date: 12/06/2012

Personal Information | Accounts | Negative Information | Inquiries

Show All Dispute Options

Step 5: Next to each entry you will see "dispute item." Click dispute item next to the place with the error. The "show details button" this will provide you all the information that you found in your credit report. Once you hit "dispute item" you will have to select a reason for the dispute. Select from the check boxes or add in your reasoning then hit "add dispute."

Select one reason from the ownership category or up to two reasons from the Account Information Category that best describes your dispute. You may not make selections from both categories.

View Ownership	Verify Account Information
☐ This account does not belong to me.	☐ My account is closed per my request to the creditor.
☐ This is not my account; it belongs to a relative or another person with same/similar name.	☐ My account is included in my bankruptcy.
☐ This is a fraudulent account;account opened by someone who stole my identity.	☐ My credit limit and/or high credit amount is incorrect.
☐ Fraudulent charges were made on my account.	☐ Please verify date of last payment, date opened, date closed, or date of first delinquency.
☐ I am no longer liable for this account.	☐ Please verify the account descriptions shown on my account.

Please use this box to provide any additional information that the creditor may use to support your dispute. You may type up to 250 characters.

Add Dispute

Step 6: Once you're done entering all your disputes. Click "Dispute Summary." Check to make sure all your disputes were captured.

Step 7: Click "Submit" and write down the confirmation number. You're going to need the dispute confirmation number to check on the status of your dispute.

Dispute by Phone:

Step 1: Get your credit report confirmation handy.
Step 2: Dial the phone number on your credit report.
Step 3: Talk to a live representative and explain what you need disputed.

Dispute by Mail:

I'll begin with the dispute department addresses for each of the three credit bureaus. They are:

Equifax
P.O. Box 7404256
Atlanta, GA 30374-0256

Experian
Dispute Department
P.O. Box 9701
Allen, TX 75013

TransUnion
Consumer Solutions
P.O. Box 2000
Chester, PA 19022-2000

Step 1: Make a copy of your credit report

Step 2: Create a dispute letter

Date
Your Name
Your Address
City, State Zip Code

Name of Company
Address
City, State Zip Code

Dear Sir or Madam:
I am writing to dispute the following information in my file. I have circled the items I dispute on the attached copy of the report I received.

This item (identify item(s) disputed by name of source, such as creditors or tax court, and identify type of item, such as credit account, judgment, etc.) is (inaccurate or incomplete) because (describe what is inaccurate or incomplete and why). I am requesting that the item be removed (or request another specific change) to correct the information.

Enclosed are copies of (use this sentence if applicable and describe any enclosed documentation, such as payment records and court documents) supporting my position. Please reinvestigate this (these) matter(s) and (delete or correct) the disputed item(s) as soon as possible.

Sincerely,
Your name

Enclosures: (List what you are enclosing.)

Step 3: Mail copy of credit report and dispute letter

That's it! Now the next step is to wait until they get back to you. This process can take up to 45 days to complete, so be patient.

Under the law, credit-reporting agencies have a number of days to investigate your claim. If they are unable to prove its accuracy, they are required to delete it from your file. This does not mean that it will remain deleted. At some point, the credit-reporting agency may receive information proving the accuracy of the disputed item. The credit-reporting agency then has the right to include it in your report, but they are also obligated to notify you in writing, within five business days, that the information is back in your report. They must also provide the name, address, and telephone number of the information provider and explain your right to add a statement to your credit file regarding the disputed information. The written statement must be 100 words or less and explain why you believe the information is inaccurate.

When the Investigation Doesn't Correct the Problem

Keep in mind, certain things need more information! You can't just change your name, address, or social security number on your credit card without proof. If you want to change your name or date of birth you need to send a copy of your driver's license reflecting the most current information. If you need to change your current address you need to send in a driver's license or a utility bill. If you need to change your social security number, you need to send in a copy of your social security card or a W2.

If the credit reporting agency determines that the information you are disputing is correct, you still have options. One option would be locating supporting documentation for your position. Make copies of everything and resubmit with your cover letter. A second option involves appealing to the original creditor or if you are one of the unlucky few, a debt collector, directly and asking that it correct the problem. Fortunately for you, this book does address handling debt collectors.

How Do I Dispute Collection Accounts?

Collection accounts have a significant impact on your credit score and every reasonable effort you can take to avoid a collection is warranted. As promised, here are the tips and tricks that you can use to get the debt collectors off your back.

The Debt Validation Game

Collection agencies are required by law to attempt to validate the debt they will attempt to collect. This process begins with a letter from the collection agency. In this letter, they should explain who they are, identify the debt they are attempting to collect, and what the balance due is on the debt. This initial letter must tell you that they will assume the debt is valid unless they hear from you to the contrary within 30 days.

ALWAYS challenge the validity of the debt even if you think it *may* be valid. While I believe it is important to challenge the debt within this 30-day window, you have the right to dispute the debt at any point in time.

SAMPLE *(Demand for Validation)*

Date:

Certified Mail, Return Receipt Requested – Certified Mail Receipt #: (21 digits)

Name of collection agency
Attn: Manager
Street or P.O. Box
City, State Zip Code

Dear Sir/Madam:

Please accept this letter as evidence that I dispute the validity of the debt described in the attached photocopy of the letter I received from your agency. I formally request that your firm verify this debt as required by the Fair Debt Collection Practices Act

I am disputing this debt because (choose one)

*I do not owe the debt
*I am a victim of identity theft
*The debt has been paid (attach proof of payment if available)
*I did not receive the service for which I was billed
*The debt is beyond the Statute of Limitations

As a result of this dispute, I understand that the Fair Credit Reporting Act precludes you from reporting this account to the credit reporting agencies. If you have already reported it, please contact the credit reporting agencies, inform them that the debt is disputed, and ask the credit reporting agencies to delete it from my credit report.

Apart from verification of the debt, I formally request that you do not contact me about this debt.

Your cooperation is appreciated.

Sincerely,

<Insert Your Name>
<Your Address>
<Your City, State Zip Code>

If you have searched for sample letters on the Internet, you will notice the letters I have included here are substantially less confrontational. This is no accident. Collectors are competitive, type-A personalities. You want to communicate that you are not a pushover while at the same time avoiding a tone that may spark these collectors to rise to a perceived challenge.

As with any written communication, I want you to maintain copies for your records.

If nothing else, this letter will delay the collection from appearing in your credit report and preclude any legal action until the collection agency provides verification of the debt. *Play the game.* You may find something additional to dispute when you receive validation from the collection agency.

On the other hand, if you actually owe the debt, you have bought yourself some time to gather the funds necessary to pay it off, nothing more. You now have to consider other options.

Pay for Delete

It is helpful for you to understand the mindset of collection agencies and the collectors who work for them. The collection agency may have purchased your account for a percentage of its face value or they may have taken your account on a commission basis. Either way, the objective is to make money. The only way they can make money is to collect at least some portion of the debt.

Collectors and the agencies they work for understand the prospects of involuntary collection from someone with an income that can't be targeted for a wage garnishment are bleak. If your sole income is social security, military retirement pay, or a federal pension, for example, they are going to be very willing to negotiate with you because even the courts cannot touch your income. You must inform the financial institution receiving your deposit that the funds are from social security, military retirement pay, or a federal pension. The bank will then be on notice not to honor any garnishment attempt. As always, I recommend you do this in writing and request written acknowledgement from your financial institution.

A small balance on the collection account also places you in a better negotiating position. There isn't a great deal to be earned on your small account and collection costs do not differ significantly between large balances and small ones. In some cases, the cost of collecting could actually exceed the amount you owe. This is your negotiating point.

The same is also true if you are in a low paying job. The collection agency can obtain a judgment and garnish your wages but they will only receive a percentage of what you earn. Obviously, the lower your earnings are, the smaller the amount they will receive, and the better your negotiating position.

Possible Outcomes

When you are negotiating with a collection agency, you can expect five possible outcomes. I recount them below in the order of preference.

1. Negotiate a settlement with the collection agency that results in the removal of the collection from your credit report(s).

2. Negotiate the removal of the collection from your credit report(s) upon full payment of the debt.

3. Negotiate a settlement that includes a "paid in full" report to the credit bureau(s), even though the collection agency has settled the debt for less than the full amount.

4. Settle the account for an amount less than is owed in exchange for a "paid-settled" report to the credit bureau(s).

5. Pay the full amount due and follow up to make sure your credit report(s) reflect the collection as paid. If the collection is not reported as paid, you will have to dispute the account and include proof of payment with your dispute letter to the credit-reporting agencies involved.

In the context above, the terms settle and settlement indicate that you have paid less than the full amount due to resolve the account. I have included a sample letter, commonly referred to as a "pay for delete" letter, to assist you. At the risk of being repetitive, send your letter by certified mail, return receipt requested, and keep copies of EVERYTHING.

SAMPLE (*Pay for delete*)

Date:

Certified Mail, Return Receipt Requested – *Certified Mail Receipt #: (21 digits)*

Re: Account Number xxx-xxxx-xx-xxxx

> *Name of collection agency*
> *Attn: Manager*
> *Street or P.O. Box*
> *City, State Zip Code*

Dear Sir/Madam:

This letter is in response to (your correspondence / our conversation / your credit report entry) on (date) regarding the above debt. I believe it is in our mutual best interests to settle this debt.

Please understand that this letter is neither an acknowledgment nor acceptance of the debt. Furthermore, this is not a payment arrangement and is not a payment agreement, unless you provide an affirmative reply as requested below.

I understand that your company has the right to submit this debt to credit reporting agencies as you see fit. I am also aware you have the ability to remove the information because you are the information provider.

I am willing to pay (this debt in full / $xxx as settlement for this debt) if you agree to remove all information with regard to this debt from the credit-reporting agencies within ten business days of payment. If you agree, I will send good funds in the amount of $xxx payable to your agency in exchange for the removal of all the information related to this debt from all of my credit reports.

If you agree to accept this offer, please state this fact in letter format on your company letterhead. This letter, over the signature of an authorized agent of your agency, will be deemed as contractually binding by each party.

Please forward the letter to the address listed below.

Sincerely,

<Insert Your Name>
<Your Address>
<Your City, State Zip Code>

Obviously, you would only send a letter like this if you have the means to act upon its acceptance. In short, you must be prepared to pay!

Night of the Living Dead

As I've said before, the collection business is highly competitive. Dare I say, "Anything for a buck?" It is common for collection agencies to purchase debt, at pennies on the dollar, that has expired and by that, I mean is beyond the statutes of limitation. These unscrupulous agencies will then attempt collection, betting that you are ignorant of the fact that the statute of limitations has expired and/or ignorant of the fact that the burden of asserting your rights under statutes of limitation is on your shoulders.

This is referred to as "phantom debt" or "zombie debt" and these agencies will try to bring it back to life through your ignorance of the law. Don't be suckered by these jerks! Know your rights!

The statute of limitations, which varies from state to state, defines the period available to the creditor to initiate legal action against you to recover the amount you owe. Statutes range from a low of three years to a high of fifteen years. The clock runs from the date of your last payment. When the clock runs out, the creditor forfeits the right to judicial remedies for recovery of the debt. In short, you cannot be sued. If the creditor attempts to sue, you *must* make an affirmative defense, citing the fact that the creditor is "time barred" from taking legal action against you pursuant to the expiration of the statute of limitations. This does not mean that a creditor cannot pursue collection efforts. It means the creditor will receive *no assistance* from the courts. It is important that you take no action that resets the clock. If you make a payment, the clock starts anew. If you sign *anything* such as an acknowledgement of the debt or an extension agreement, the clock starts all over again.

Goodwill Hunting

Sometimes it is simply not possible to have negative information removed from your credit file. Let's face it, shit happens! We all run into to unavoidable situations that can result in negative information appearing on our credit reports, information that is factual and cannot be successfully disputed. In such circumstances, it is worth your time and effort to consider appealing to the 'better angels" that occasionally reside within those hard-nosed creatures that wander the halls of our financial institutions. I refer to the "goodwill letter."

Although I am including a sample letter, it is important for you to understand that any such letter is unique to your circumstances and to your relationship with the target credit provider.

I suggest that you avoid "sob stories," pointed requests to change your file and above all, accept responsibility for your shortcomings. Anyone in the business of lending has heard it all … twice! It is preferable to base your appeal on the strength of your business relationship, their sense of fairness etc.

The sample below should give you a starting point for composing your personalized appeal for justice.

Sample Good Will Letter

Date:

Certified Mail, Return Receipt Requested – Certified Mail Receipt #: (21 digits)

Re: Account number xxx-xxx-xx-xxxx

Name of creditor / financial institution
Attn: Credit Manager
Street or P.O. Box
City, State Zip Code

Dear Sir/Madam:

As you may be aware, my account reflects late payments in the first quarter of this year. While this information is accurately reflected in my credit file with TransUnion / Equifax / Experian (name all that apply), I feel compelled to explain the reason these delinquencies occurred.

I am, or I should say, was an employee of XYZ Corporation. Late last year, my position was eliminated in a corporate downsizing. Regrettably, I was inadequately prepared financially to deal with this, as it was rather unexpected. I certainly should have recognized the warning signs but, unfortunately, I did not.

As my records reflect, I have enjoyed a long relationship with your firm, and I hope you will agree that, for the greater part, it has been mutually rewarding and satisfactory to all concerned.

I need not tell you the very negative impact these delinquencies are having on me financially.

Given our longstanding and largely satisfactory business relationship, I am wondering if you might be in a position to offer some advice or suggest a possible solution to this vexing problem.

Anything you can offer by way of assistance will be very much appreciated.

Respectfully,

<Insert Your Name>
<Your Address>
<Your City, State, Zip>

I offer no guarantees, of course, but such letters, although rarely answered, often result in the mysterious removal of adverse information from the sender's credit report.

The Law Is on Your Side

This section will be devoted to a synopsis of your rights as defined by the Fair Credit Reporting Act and the Credit Card Act of 2009. These are the two principal pieces of legislation, which make it possible for you to fight the good credit fight. When healing your credit, it is important to know your rights.

The Fair Credit Reporting Act gives you the right to:

- Have inaccurate information in your credit record corrected and outdated information deleted if a credit bureau investigation finds the information to be in error

- Have information deleted if the credit bureau cannot verify it through its investigation within 30 days of receiving your investigation request

- Know the name, address, and phone number of anyone who has seen your credit record over the past two years for employment purposes and the right to know who has reviewed your credit information for any other purpose over the past 12 months

- Have a credit bureau notify employers who reviewed your credit record over the past two years, or anyone else who may have reviewed your file over the previous six months, of any corrections or deletions made to your credit file, if you so request and provide the credit-reporting agency the names of all companies and individuals you want notified

- Have a brief explanatory statement added to credit file with regard to information in your file that you dispute but have been unsuccessful in changing or deleting

- Have most negative credit related information deleted from your credit record after seven years

- To have a bankruptcy deleted after ten years

- Sue a credit bureau in either state or federal court if it willfully or negligently violates the law

- Be notified by a company that it has requested an investigative report on you

- Request from a company pursuing an investigative report more information about the nature and scope of the investigation

The CARD Act of 2009

The role the CARD Act of 2009 plays in credit repair is *indirect* in nature. Rather than giving you a mechanism for challenging the credit-reporting agencies, it acts as "preventative medicine" by guaranteeing you equitable treatment and some ability to control their own destiny. In short, the act will make it less likely for you to get into credit card debt because of abusive practices by credit card issuers. Below, I list the key provisions of the act.

Stops Surprise Rate Increases and Changes in Terms

- No more indiscriminate interest rate hikes or universal default on your credit card simply because you were late on another debt

- If your rate is increased for cause (such as a 60-day delinquency), the credit card company must review your payment record periodically and adjust the rate to its previous level if you have made your payments on time for six months

- Credit card issuers cannot increase your rates in the first year

- Promotional rates are permitted, but must remain in force for a minimum of six months

- Rates and terms may be changed, but a 45-day notice is required

Prohibits Unnecessary Fees

- Card issuers are no longer permitted to charge you a fee to pay a credit card debt, by mail, telephone, or electronic transfer, the exception being live services to make rush payments

- Over-limit fees are banned unless you choose to allow the issuer to complete over-limit transactions, and even if you do, the act limits these fees to one per billing cycle

- Penalty fees must be reasonable and proportional to the transgression

- Improved protections against exorbitant fees on low limit, high-fee credit cards

Requires Consumer Oriented Application and Timing of Card Payments

- If you pay more than your minimum payment, the excess must be applied first to the credit card balance with the highest rate of interest (typically the cash advance balance)

- Card issuers cannot set early morning deadlines for payments

- Statements must be mailed 21 days before the due

No More "Double-Cycle" Billing

- Stops the dubious practice of basing finance charges on the average balance over two billing cycles, which penalizes you if you pay your balance in full

- Prohibits late fees caused by delays in crediting your payment

- Payments made at local branches must be credited same-day

- Mandates that credit card companies evaluate your ability to pay before issuing your credit card or raising your credit limit

Requires Improved Disclosure of Credit Terms and Conditions

- Mandates that you be given 45 days' notice of interest rate, fee, and finance charge increases

- Disclosures must be provided upon your card's renewal if terms have changed

- Credit card companies must disclose the length of time to retire your debt and total interest expense that results from making only the minimum payment

- Each billing statement must disclose payment due dates and applicable late payment fees

Makes Industry Practices More Transparent

- Card issuers must make their credit card agreements available on the Internet, and furnish those agreements to the Federal Reserve Board, which will also publish them on their website

- The Federal Reserve Board is required to review the consumer credit card market, the terms of credit card agreements, the practices of credit card issuers, and the cost and availability of credit to consumers

- Mandates the Federal Trade Commission to prevent the deceptive marketing of so-called free credit reports

Precludes the Exploitation of Young People

- Persons under the age of twenty-one must prove their ability to pay or provide a co-signer aged 21 or older to or their credit card application will not be approved

- Limits prescreened offers of credit to persons under 21 years of age

- Credit limit increases on co-signed accounts must also be approved by the person jointly responsible for the debt

Provides for Higher Penalties

- Implements more severe penalties for any company violating the Truth in Lending Act for credit card customers

Gift Card Rules

- Mandates that gift cards be valid for five years and eliminates the practice of graduated reductions in card value and hidden fees

Protects Entrepreneurs

- The Federal Reserve is required to study the use of credit cards by small businesses and make recommendations for regulatory and legislative changes

- The act establishes Small Business Information Security Task Force to address the information technology security needs of small business and develop measures to prevent the loss of credit card data

Mandates Financial Literacy

- Mandates the development of a comprehensive plan to improve financial literacy education and the summarization of existing financial literacy initiatives

It is *always* a good idea to include a copy of your credit report with any correspondence you send to a credit-reporting agency with the error(s) highlighted or circled.

Avoid including anything in your correspondence that is unprofessional or frivolous in nature. The credit reporting agencies can reject frivolous disputes. However, the credit reporting agency must inform you in writing of their refusal to investigate and include an explanation of why it views your request as frivolous or irrelevant. Maintaining a business-like approach will add credibility to your allegations of inaccuracies.

Protecting Your Credit

Imagine this scenario. You have always paid your bills on time. Literally, you've never missed a payment. In your mind, you should have perfect credit. Then one day out of the blue, you begin to get phone calls from collection agencies calling you a dead beat and demanding money for a bunch of past-due accounts that you know for a fact that you never opened.

The timing of all this could not be any worse! You just started to look at houses to buy and had an appointment with a realtor that weekend to check out that great neighborhood with the good schools. Now your bank is going to think you're a risky borrower and will most likely refuse to give you a mortgage, or if they do decide to let you move forward with the process, it's going to cost you a lot of money in the form of a ridiculously high interest rate. That's not the worst of it either, and now the IRS is now sending letters saying you owe income taxes on money you never seen!

Now you're sitting there thinking, "How could all of this have happened?" Well, truthfully it happens all the time. You're a victim of identity theft, a crime that affects millions of people a year. You know what happened right? Some a-hole employee in the hospital, dentist's office, or your HR department stole your social security number and sold it for a few bucks. Your social security number was then used to open credit cards, get auto loans, rent apartments, sign up for utilities, and even to earn income in your name.

The sad thing is that it takes seconds to get your identity stolen, but it takes years to get the credit bureaus to fix your credit report, all while the thief is probably living it up, all on your dime, and guess what? The creditors will still harass you!

Sources of Identity Theft

Did you know that most identity theft occurs offline and by your friends, relatives, and other people you know? Do me a favor and write down five of your closest family members and friends. If your identity is going to get stolen, it is probably going to be a person on that list. I bet you would have thought that most of theft occurs online via sophisticated computer hacks. I'm sure that in the future thieves will move to more sophisticated computer hacking for stealing your identity, but until that day comes…watch your friends.

How Identity Robbers Maneuver

So, we know who the identity thieves are, but how do they operate? Identity thieves range from old-school pickpockets to complex theft rings. All they really need is a little personal information, and they are in business. To help accumulate your private information, ID-theft rings get cleaning people (that recover records from their workplace wastebaskets), corrupt companies (that sell credit-card sales receipts), and workers of bank and brokerage backroom operations that process transactions. Just what are they looking for? Anything that will lead them to the one piece of info they need to take your identity like your Social Security number! Online, there are several sorts of high-level identity theft techniques, including "phishing" and "pharming." According to security exports, phishing attacks use "spoofed" e-mails and bogus sites created to deceive you into revealing private financial data such as credit card numbers, account usernames, passwords, Social Security numbers, and so on. Pharming makes use of the exact same kind of spoofed internet sites, yet makes use of malware and spyware to redirect individuals from genuine sites to the fraudulent sites (normally DNS hijacking). By hijacking the trusted labels of popular financial institutions and merchants, phishers have the ability to encourage you to answer to them.

Are You At Risk?

It ought to come as no surprise that crooks target those with the most to lose. That's why credit worthy people with excellent incomes are commonly victims of identity theft scams. Other prospective victims include people who share the exact same name such as Juniors, Seniors, or other relatives. Identity thieves like to exploit the confusion over similar names to acquire your personal information.

How Do Criminals Get Social Security Numbers?

When criminals have a name, acquiring the Social Security number is the following action. According to authorities, identification theft rings sometimes pay low-level staff members of the Social Security Administration or Internal Revenue Service to obtain the numbers. Numerous states use Social Security numbers as your driver's license number and guess what, driving records are public files, and the number is effortless to get. Schools, healthcare facilities, and the IRS like to use Social Security numbers as your identifier.

Credit Bureaus and some other records providers may unsuspectingly provide the identity thieves with your social security number. How? Well you can buy access to the credit bureaus credit records, matter of fact it's part of their business model to sell credit records. Genuine companies typically get this sort of access from the credit agency to examine potential clients. The problem is the sale of your credit records by the credit bureaus is not controlled by any federal laws and, as a result, is at risk for scams.

Take a look at your mail, in a month's time you probably run across your social security number a few times without even notice it. All a thief would need to do is file a temporary address change with the post office and, this will allow them to send your mail to the location of their choice for 30 days. You probably won't even notice it, before the temporary address change wears off. Another thing that you may not be aware of is that you probably get a lot of credit solicitation offers. If I have your mail, I can easily open one of those credit card offers in your name.

Fortunately, improved efforts have actually been made to stop the over-use of consumers' Social Security numbers as an identifier for accounts. Healthcare service providers, schools, and other institutions now release their own sort of identifiers in order to recognize group members.

What Can You Do To Protect Yourself?

After hearing all the bad news on who, how, and why people want your identity, I think it's fitting that I give you some steps to protect yourself.

- One of the main things you want to do is opt out of all pre-screen offers. You can do that my going here: http://www.optoutprescreen.com/

- Get a cross-cut shredder. The best way to keep thieves from getting your personal information is to shred it. All your old bills, unwanted credit and insurance offers and anything with your personal information should be shredded.

- Go digital. If you pay your bills online and get statements via email, you don't have to shred anything, but you need to make sure you have strong user name and passwords for all your digital accounts.

- Use an Alert, a Freeze, or Credit monitoring. I go over this in more detail and give you the step by step process in the following sections.

- Watch out for change of address notifications. The USA Postal Service recently modified its change-of-address procedures to combat identity burglars. Now, after a post office obtains a change-of-address request, it delivers a verification letter to the old address. If you get such a notice and did not ask for the modification, contact your neighborhood post office right away.

- Request a new license number. If you live in a state that utilizes your Social Security Number as ID number, ask for a different number.

- Do not provide personal information when writing a check.

- Review your credit reports!

Protect Your Credit: Fraud Alert

In addition to healing your credit, you need to protect it as well because there is nothing worse than having to deal with credit card fraud and identity theft. A fraud alert on your credit report is one step you can take to protect yourself.

What is a Fraud Alert?

A fraud alert is a notation on your credit report to potential creditors that you suspect you are or have been a victim of identity theft. This notation appears right there on your credit report. Here's what happens: Within 24 to 48 hours of you placing a fraud alert on your credit report, it will show up on all of your credit reports from the big three reporting agencies: TransUnion,

Experian, and Equifax. This notation is intended to alert potential lenders that you should be contacted to verify you are actually the person requesting new or expanded credit.

The Three Types of Fraud Alerts

Initial 90 Day Fraud Alert

The 90 day fraud alert (also referred to as an Initial Security Alert) is exactly like it sounds. It is a 90 day notation on your credit report. This notation indicates that you are concerned about new credit being requested in your name. The 90 day fraud alert is set up to work like this: if the Credit Reporting Agency receives a request from any potential lender for new credit or even a credit line increase for existing creditors, they are supposed to contact you to verify the request. If the potential lenders are unable to contact you or they are otherwise unable to verify this request, they are not supposed to move forward. Please note that this is the intent of a fraud alert. However, be aware that there is no law stipulating that potential lenders must honor this fraud alert in your credit report. Also, note that at the end of 90 days, the fraud alert expires and is no longer active. At that point, if you wish to reactivate the fraud alert past the 90 day period, you will need to complete the process again. One side benefit of installing a 90 Day Fraud Alert is that it entitles you to one more free credit report.

Extended Fraud Alert

The extended fraud alert is very similar to the Initial 90 Day Fraud Alert with some important differences. The most notable difference is that this option is only available to verified victims of identity theft. Whereas the initial 90 day fraud alert is available to anyone at any time, you must prove you are an identity theft victim to obtain an extended fraud alert. When you send in your request with the credit reporting agency, in most cases, you will need a valid report from your local law enforcement department.

Another key difference with the extended fraud alert is time. The extended fraud alert lasts for seven years unless removed by you beforehand. A third difference between the 90 day fraud alert and the extended fraud alert is the specific contact requirements from new or existing creditors. The extended fraud alert requires creditors to contact you via the telephone number you provide to the Credit Reporting Agency when you request this fraud alert. Finally, yet another difference with the extended fraud alert is your name is dropped from certain lists. That means that along with the extended fraud alert status, your name will be removed from those pre-screened credit or insurance company offers. You should note, however, that even though the extended fraud alert lasts for seven years, you are only removed from these pre-screened offers for five years. One additional benefit you receive with an extended fraud alert is that it entitles you to two more free credit reports.

Active Duty Alert

The active duty alert is intended for those members of the Armed Forces on active duty. The Active Duty Alert is much like the Initial 90 Day Fraud Alert with two significant differences.

1. The active duty alert status lasts for 12 months instead of 90 days.
2. Installing an Active Duty alert removes your name form prescreened credit or insurance offers for two years.

What Happens When You Put a Fraud Alert on Your Credit Report?

The process begins once you contact any of the three credit reporting agencies. You should note that in the case of a fraud alert, you only need to contact one agency. It does not matter which credit reporting agency you contact because the other two agencies will automatically be notified of your request.

After you contact one of the big three credit reporting agencies, your fraud alert will become activated. Within twenty-four hours of your initial notification, your fraud alert should be active at all three credit reporting agencies. Later you will receive a confirmation of your request for a fraud alert by postal mail service. Next, your name is removed from pre-screened offer lists. These lists are the source of all that junk mail about new credit cards or special finance deals.

Finally, your countdown clock starts counting. Since a fraud alert expires in 90 days, the credit reporting agencies have it set up for expiration at the end of day 90. Of course, if you have set up and extended fraud alert or an active duty alert, you have a different clock.

Advantages

The biggest advantage to putting a fraud alert on your credit report is at least some level of protection against new credit or expanded credit being obtained in your name. A secondary benefit is one more free credit report. An unusual benefit you may enjoy is much less junk mail since your name will be taken off those lists.

Disadvantages

The biggest disadvantage with using a fraud alert is the false sense of security you may feel. You must understand that a fraud alert is not a cure-all solution for identity theft concerns. A second disadvantage to putting a fraud alert on your credit report is lack of enforcement. The fact is that there is no legal requirement for a lender to contact you with the 90 day fraud alert. Although it is probably true that the larger creditors will at least make some sort of attempt, there is no guarantee that they will. The extended fraud alert, however, requires the lender to contact you by telephone.

Steps to Put a Fraud Alert on Your Credit Report

Step 1: Evaluate both the advantages and disadvantages to putting a fraud alert on your credit report. You want to make an informed decision.

Step 2: Determine what type of fraud alert applies to your situation. Will you be asking for an Initial 90 Day Fraud Alert, an Extended Fraud Alert, or an Active Duty Fraud Alert?

Step 3: Contact any one of the big three Credit Reporting Agencies. Follow their procedures online or call them directly, and they will walk you through the necessary steps. Also, keep in mind, to install a 90 Day Fraud Alert on your credit report you should only have to notify just one reporting agency. However, be aware that there will be documentation requirements for both the Extended Fraud Alert and the Active Duty Fraud Alert notifications.

The Credit Reporting Agency contact phone numbers and websites are listed here below.

TRANSUNION	EXPERIAN	EQUIFAX
Phone: 1-888-909-8872	Phone: 1-888-397-3742	Phone: 1-888-766-0008
Web: www.transunion.com	Web: www.experian.com	Web: www.equifax.com

Step 4: After requesting a fraud alert, you should receive a confirmation in the mail. If you do not receive your confirmation within one to two weeks, contact the credit reporting agency again. You want to deal with the agency where you initially made your fraud alert request. Find out if the fraud alert was actually put into effect. If the fraud alert was put in place, ask about your confirmation. In some cases, you may have to start all over and request a new fraud alert.

Step 5: Consider setting up a reminder for yourself if you believe you will need to renew your fraud alert. Keep in mind that unless you take an active stance and remember to reinstate your 90 Day Fraud Alert, it will expire. Of course, the Extended Fraud Alert and the Active Duty Fraud Alert have different expiration dates. Also, be aware of timing hazards. This means that should your fraud alert expire, and there is a delay before you reinstate it, your credit report will not show a fraud alert to interested parties.

Step 6: (Optional) Remember that if you have verifiable evidence of real or even attempted attempts to steal your identity, you have another choice. You can choose the option of getting an Extended Fraud Alert. One significant advantage offered by the Extended Fraud Alert is that it lasts for seven years.

Protect Your Credit: Credit Freeze

Many consider a credit freeze (also known as a security freeze) to be the ultimate weapon in the fight against identity theft. A credit freeze does offer a measure of protection for the information in your credit report. However, as you will soon see there are both advantages and disadvantages to freezing your credit.

What is a Credit Freeze?

A credit freeze can be compared to putting a deadbolt lock on your door at home. Like the deadbolt lock, consider a credit freeze as a sort of lock-down on your credit report. This lock down keeps your credit report away from prying eyes. Consider that some who gain access to your credit report may want to use your information for malicious purposes. A credit freeze is setup by you and the credit reporting agencies to deny access to your credit report. You may or may not be surprised to learn that the identity theft experts report that approximately 15% of identity theft cases arise from malicious use of credit report information. With this statistic in mind, now you can better understand the motivation to freeze your credit.

Credit Freeze Specifics

- The credit freeze does not apply to everyone. A fundamental reality you must understand is that the denial of access to your credit report does not apply to existing creditor relationships. For example, your existing mortgage company and credit card companies will still have access to your credit report. Additionally, in some states, potential employers, potential landlords, or potential insurance companies also continue to have access to your credit report.

- The credit freeze law will not shield you from collection companies. If any of your existing creditor relationships has been sent to collections, that collections firm still has access to your credit report.

- Credit freeze laws depend on where you live. Unlike a fraud alert or other consumer credit protection requirements available from the Fair Credit Reporting Act, a credit freeze is not a federal law. Instead, each state has or has not passed its own credit freeze statues. This means you need to check your own state first for the exact requirements. Alternatively, you may contact any of the big three credit reporting agencies, and they will assist you in freezing your credit.

- Freezing your credit has zero effect on your credit score. As you probably know, a credit score is based on a proprietary formula which does not consider credit freeze as a positive or negative factor.

- The credit freeze lasts as long as you want. You decide when or if to ever unfreeze your credit. One factor you will want to consider when you are contemplating a credit freeze is your need for new credit. For example, a young college graduate just starting his first new job is more likely to be applying for more credit more often. Alternatively, a retired senior living on her state pension and savings is less likely to need new credit that often. From this example you can see that the credit freeze may be a no-brainer for the retired senior. Alternatively, the new college graduate has an entirely different perspective.

- The credit freeze is not free. In fact, the fees are literally all over the map. Since each state has passed its own credit freeze law, each state sets their own fee structure. However, note that credit freeze statues in most states allow for a free credit freeze for proven victims of identity theft. Proving you are a victim of identity theft most often means providing a copy of the identity theft report you filed with your local law enforcement department.

- Unfreezing your credit is not free either. As of now, all three credit reporting agencies are charging for unfreezing your credit. Note these fees apply for each unfreeze you request. Also, be aware that these fees can add up over time. For example, let's go back to our young college graduate. If his credit report was frozen, he would need to pay to unfreeze his credit report when he is ready to move into a new apartment in the happening part of the city next to his new job. Then, he will have to unfreeze his credit again when he applies for a new car loan. Perhaps even one more time, if he is ambitious and applies for a new credit card to go along with his new job. At the end of the year, he will have paid each credit reporting agency three times each to unfreeze his credit report temporarily.

- A credit freeze must be requested individually from each credit reporting agency. Unlike a fraud alert where notifying one credit agency means the other agencies are notified automatically, the credit freeze is a separate activity you must perform with each credit reporting agency.

What Happens When You Freeze Your Credit Report?

As mentioned above, as soon as you begin the credit freeze, the credit reporting agencies put your credit report on lock down. What this means that as soon as your credit report is frozen, the credit reporting agencies stop releasing your credit information. Next, the credit reporting agencies will issue you a personal identification number (PIN). You will also receive a password to be used with your PIN. You will need both of these should you need to unfreeze your credit report temporarily.

For example, let's say you wish to move into a new apartment downtown. In many locations, it is standard policy for potential landlords to request a credit report as a condition of leasing. In order to provide this credit report, you will of course have to unfreeze your credit report temporarily. Here's another way to look at it. Go back to the analogy of your deadbolt lock. The potential landlord is a like a trusted friend that you invite over for a cup of tea. So, when your friend comes over, you slide the deadbolt aside for a minute to let her inside. Later after your friend leaves, you quickly bolt the door locked again. Can you see how this works now? The credit freeze allows you selective invitations to potential creditors to view your credit report.

Advantages

The greatest advantage to freezing is that your credit report truly is on lockdown. With a credit freeze in place, it is virtually impossible for someone to obtain credit in your name. Remember, the credit freeze keeps your credit report away from everyone, but especially those who are up to no good. As mentioned above, identity theft experts report that about 15% of identity theft cases arise from credit obtained in someone else's name. Another advantage with a credit report freeze is that you will get a whole lot less junk mail. Your name should not show up on those pre-approved credit mailers anymore.

Disadvantages

There are a few disadvantages to freezing your credit report. For one thing, you will have to say good bye to instant credit opportunities. For example, suppose you are holiday shopping at Macy's, and they offer you a free gift to apply for a store card. With a credit freeze in place, instant approval is not an option. In fact, it may take up to three days to temporarily unfreeze your credit report.

Another disadvantage of the credit freeze is that it can be somewhat difficult to remove. Remember, to unfreeze your account, you must have your PIN number and your password handy. Finally, another disadvantage to the credit report freeze is a false sense of security. The credit freeze can stop some forms of identity theft, but it is not a 100% guarantee. Remember, the credit experts themselves report that 15% of identity theft arises from stolen credit information. That leaves 85% of identity theft cases caused by other factors. You would not want to put a credit freeze in place and ignore the other identity theft precautions.

Steps to Freezing Your Credit

Step 1: Evaluate both the advantages and disadvantages to freezing your credit.

Step 2: Contact each credit reporting agency separately. Remember to freeze your credit you must do it at each reporting agency. The contact phone numbers and websites are listed below.

TRANSUNION	EXPERIAN	EQUIFAX
Phone: 1-888-909-8872	Phone: 1-888-397-3742	Phone: 1-888-766-0008
Web: www.transunion.com	Web: www.experian.com	Web: www.equifax.com

Step 3: Carefully record each personal identification number (PIN) for each credit reporting agency. Also, make sure you know or record the password associated with each PIN. Remember, you will need this PIN and password combination should you need to unfreeze your credit.

Protect Your Credit: Credit Monitoring

In addition to fraud alerts and credit freezes, you can invest in credit monitoring to protect your credit. This is an entirely new industry, the credit monitoring service, which has arisen in the past few years offering to protect your personal financial information.

What is Credit Monitoring?

Credit monitoring means monitoring and inspecting your credit history as shown on your credit report. In the end, that's really what it's all about, your credit report, and more importantly unexpected changes to your credit report. A credit monitoring service provides this monitoring service for you (for a fee, of course). Most credit monitoring services report that they monitor and track your credit report daily.

What Happens with Credit Monitoring?

Once you sign up with a credit monitoring company, they pull all your information from all three credit reporting agencies. Next, they typically ask if you are in the process of applying for new credit. Often they will ask you to review the credit report and verify the information. Of course, they will want to know about any activity you consider suspicious. Now, your new credit monitoring service has a baseline or starting point. Any changes to your credit report going forward could be flagged as possibly fraudulent. Depending on the options available and the monitoring plan you chose, you will be alerted to any suspicious activity that could affect your credit report.

The credit monitoring companies typically are on the alert for:

- New credit inquiries
- Delinquencies
- Negative information that suddenly shows up
- Employment changes
- New credit accounts
- Increased credit lines at existing accounts
- Other changes to your credit report that could be considered a red flag for identity theft

You should note that one reason credit monitoring services have become so popular lately is their alerts for suspicious activity on your credit report is viewed as a counter to identity theft. Some credit monitoring companies even promote their services with this claim.

Advantages

- Constant Tracking - All of your credit reports are constantly tracked. Depending on your choice of credit monitoring companies and plans, this monitoring could be daily or weekly.

- Increased Knowledge - about your own credit. During the time you use a credit monitoring service, you will gain an incredibly valuable firsthand knowledge of how personal credit actually works. Simply by watching the reports provided from your credit monitoring service, you will see in real time how your credit report changes. You will see how even small actions on your part can have a sizeable effect on your credit score. For example, you can watch your credit score drop right after you applied for four different department store credit cards.

- It Doesn't Cost, it Saves - Yes, this is a tired old cliché, yet here it truly works. Consider it this way: suppose you use your new knowledge of how your personal credit works, how small things affect your credit score, and that sort of thing to get a better loan rate. Really, it is that easy. For example, let's say you use your new found credit wisdom to raise your credit score by 75 points. Then, you refinance your home and get a lower interest rate that saves you hundreds of dollars a month or thousands of dollars over the term of your mortgage.

- Identity Theft Protection - Since your credit report is under constant scrutiny, detection of possible fraudulent activity happens much faster. The credit monitoring service helps you both detect and minimize damage from malicious use of your personal financial information. Additionally, many credit monitoring companies offer legal protections and financial reimbursements. These reimbursements can range from $25,000 to $1,000,000.

Surely you have seen the advertisements with the big name credit monitoring service offering their one million dollar guarantee.

- <u>Faster Resolution of Errors</u> - Should you spot an error on one of your many reports sent to you by your credit monitoring service, most of them will assist you in correcting the error.

- <u>No More Guesswork</u> - Since you are paying for professional credit monitoring, you don't have to guess what is going on with your credit score or your credit report. Additionally, since your credit monitoring service will alert you for any suspicious activities, you are always aware of what's happening with your credit.

- <u>Less Hassle for You</u> - Yes, credit monitoring can be done yourself as will be explained shortly. However, paying for a credit monitoring service eliminates one more thing for you to do.

Disadvantages

- <u>Price</u> - Of course, all of the services provided by credit monitoring companies comes at a price. Price is one common complaint against credit monitoring companies. Each company sets their own pricing structure. Also, many of them offer different levels of service at different price points.

- <u>Information Disparity</u> - The information available from one credit monitoring service can be vastly different from another credit monitoring service. Make sure you know what you are paying for when you sign up for a credit monitoring plan.

- <u>Cancellation Issues</u> - There are various reports (complaints) from past customers of some credit monitoring services regarding the difficulty encountered in cancelling the service. Before you sign up for a credit monitoring plan, check out some user reviews.

- <u>Micromanagement Time Wastes</u> - Because your new credit monitoring service provides you with frequent reports and analysis, you may end up trying to micromanage your credit score. This micromanagement could end up costing you a lot of time with few, if any, substantive changes to your credit score.

- <u>False Sense of Security</u> - Since you are paying for a credit monitoring service, the tendency is to fall into the trap of that's all you need to do to protect yourself. Identity theft protection involves additional areas beyond your credit report that you still need to monitor.

- <u>A Credit Monitoring Service Can't Do it as Fast as You Might Want</u> - It is not yet possible to monitor a person's credit history on a real time basis. For one thing, many creditors only report information on existing clients weekly or even monthly.

- A Credit Monitoring Service is not the Final Solution - Even the very best credit monitoring service is not capable of fully identifying all fraudulent activity. Consider that there are many credit details that are never even reported to a credit reporting agency.

Monitoring Your Credit Report Yourself

You should remember you can always inspect your credit report yourself. One good strategy for do-it-yourselfers is to stagger your free credit reports. For example, simply order one free credit report from the first credit reporting agency. Then, four months later, repeat the process with a second credit reporting agency. If you keep following this staggered pattern, by the end of the year, you will have three free credit reports spaced four months apart.

If you do choose the self-monitoring option, there are some strategies you can use. Actually, you will see that you can use many of the same techniques the credit monitoring services employ if you are willing to be a little bit hands-on. For example, you can use the fraud alert and the credit freeze.

What to Do if Your Identity is Stolen

1. Place a fraud alert on your credit report.
2. Order your credit report and dispute everything.
3. Create an identity theft report.

We covered numbers 1 and 2. Let's cover number 3

Create an Identity Theft Report

An Identity Theft Report helps you deal with credit reporting companies, debt collectors, and businesses that opened accounts in your name. You can use the report to:

- Get fraudulent information removed from your credit report
- Stop a company from collecting debts that result from identity theft or from selling the debt to another company for collection
- Place an extended fraud alert on your credit report
- Get information from companies about accounts the identity thief opened or misused

Creating an Identity Theft Report in 3 Steps

1. Submit a complaint about the theft to the FTC. When you finish writing all the details, print a copy of the report. It will print as an Identity Theft Affidavit.

2. File a police report about the identity theft, and get a copy of the police report or the report number. Bring your FTC Identity Theft Affidavit when you file a police report.

3. Attach your FTC Identity Theft Affidavit to your police report to make an Identity Theft Report.

Some companies want more information than the Identity Theft Report includes or want different information. The information you need to provide depends on the policies of the credit reporting company and the business that sent the information about you to the credit reporting company.

Now You Know

Now you know nearly everything there is to know about your credit. You know how to get a credit report, and you know what that report contains. You know the steps you need to take in order to dispute any errors on those report. You know your rights, and you know how to deal with debt collectors. You also know the various tools that you can use to protect yourself from identity theft, and you know what to do if you are a victim of identity theft.

All of these things help you to improve your credit score and to keep it high. When you are well-educated, it is much easier for you to have good credit, and as you read, good credit opens the door to a variety of opportunities in life.

BONUS CONTENT

HOW TO FIX YOUR CREDIT IN 60 DAYS!

This guide will give you the step-by-step blueprint on how to repair your credit! Let's get right into it.

1. Pull your credit report.
2. Review your credit report for errors (highlight it).
3. Dispute incorrect names, addresses, SSN and date of birth first and do so via certified mail.

Supporting documentation is needed for some disputes, such as name, address, and updates to your Social Security number. You will be asked to submit the below information if you dispute personal identification information online.

- If you report an inaccuracy or change to your name or date of birth, you will need to send them a copy of your driver's license reflecting this change.

- If you report an inaccuracy or change to your current address, you will need to send them a copy of your driver's license or a utility bill reflecting this change.

- If you report an inaccuracy to your social security number, you will need to send them a copy of your social security card or a W-2 form.

Addresses for Credit Bureaus

Experian
P.O. Box 2002
Allen, TX 75013

Equifax Credit Information Services, Inc.
P.O. Box 740256
Atlanta, GA 30374

TransUnion, LLC
P.O. Box 2000
Chester, PA 19022

4. Dispute/validate everything else via the method below including when:
   a. You're disputing information via the credit bureaus
   b. You're validating debt via the collection agency

Follow the following diagram to execute the Mass Credit Attack repair strategy! Keep in mind you're sending letters to the credit reporting agencies and debt collectors at the same time!

60 DAY CREDIT REPAIR ROAD MAP

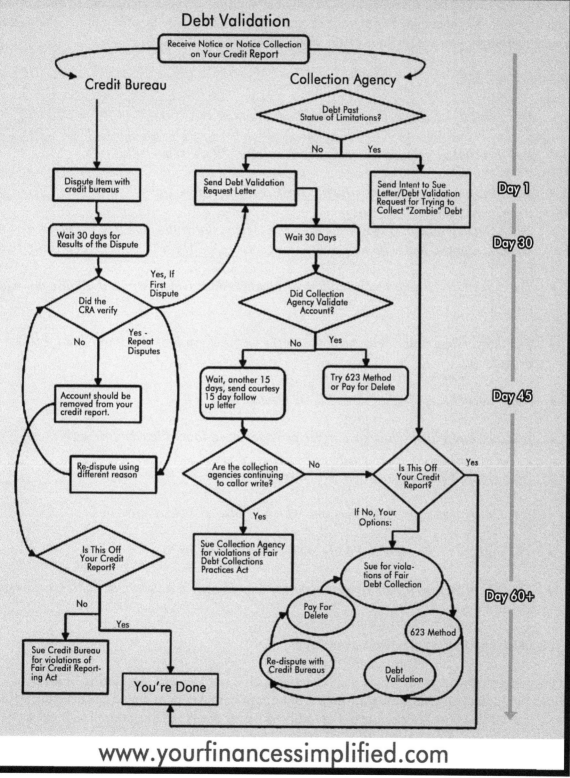

Debt Validation

Receive Notice or Notice Collection on Your Credit Report

Credit Bureau

Collection Agency

Debt Past Statue of Limitations?
No — Yes

Dispute Item with credit bureaus

Send Debt Validation Request Letter

Send Intent to Sue Letter/Debt Validation Request for Trying to Collect "Zombie" Debt — Day 1

Wait 30 days for Results of the Dispute

Wait 30 Days — Day 30

Yes, If First Dispute

Did the CRA verify
No — Yes - Repeat Disputes

Did Collection Agency Validate Account?
No — Yes

Account should be removed from your credit report.

Wait, another 15 days, send courtesy 15 day follow up letter

Try 623 Method or Pay for Delete — Day 45

Re-dispute using different reason

Are the collection agencies continuing to call or write?
No — Is This Off Your Credit Report? — Yes

If No, Your Options:

Is This Off Your Credit Report?
No — Yes

Yes

Sue Collection Agency for violations of Fair Debt Collections Practices Act

Sue for violations of Fair Debt Collection

Pay For Delete

623 Method — Day 60+

Sue Credit Bureau for violations of Fair Credit Reporting Act

You're Done

Re-dispute with Credit Bureaus

Debt Validation

www.yourfinancessimplified.com

53

What to Send to the Credit Bureau

The credit bureau employees are on a time limit per dispute. It seems that every time a consumer says "not mine" or "no records," it gets verified quickly due to the address and name match up. So, it was discovered that if you're going to dispute anything on your credit report, and you hope to get it removed, you cannot be vague. You can't simply say, "Hey this isn't mine." You need to dispute everything you see on your credit report, even the small things.

Something like this:

- *This is not a data factoring account. Please remove this.*

- *It is reported as an open account, which is false. Please remove this.*

- *It reports a one-month term which is false. Please remove this.*

- *The estimated date of removal for the CA does not match the date that the original creditor reports. The original creditor is reporting 9/2010. Please correct or remove this.*

- *The date of first delinquency with the original creditor is not provided. Please provide this.*

- *The date of first major delinquency with the original creditor is not provided. Please provide this.*

- *It has never been 120 days late. Please remove this.*

- *It is listed as a loan. They have never provided me a loan. Please remove this.*

- *No payment was made in 2/2007. Please remove this.*

- *It is listed as an installment account, which is false. Please remove this.*

- *The balance is not correct. Please correct or remove this.*

- *The end of the seven year reporting period should be listed as 09/2010. Please correct or remove this.*

If you add even MORE trade lines, even better!

So the concept is when you write a dispute letter spell it out like this, requesting SPECIFIC actions per individually listed item, which will hopefully make them delete because the problems are so in error that they are obviously flagrantly violating the law. Don't forget to break down the ENTIRE trade line. You **have** to state what you want the outcome to be.

Do you see how the example above says "Please remove this" after every sentence?

What to Send to the Collection Agency

When a collection agency is assigned, or has purchased, your debt, they are NOT the creditor. They are the debt collector, and the actions they take are all governed by the FDCPA.

You send the collection agency a debt validation (via certified mail) letter like this:

Date

Your Name
Your Address
City, State Zip Code

Collection Agency
Collection Agency Address
City, State Zip Code

Re: Acct # XXXX-XXXX-XXXX-XXXX

To Whom It May Concern:

I am sending this letter to you in response to a notice I received from you on (date of letter). Be advised, this is not a refusal to pay, but a notice sent pursuant to the Fair Debt Collection Practices Act, 15 USC 1692g Sec. 809 (b) that your claim is disputed and validation is requested.

This is NOT a request for "verification" or proof of my mailing address, but a request for VALIDATION made pursuant to the above named Title and Section. I respectfully request that your office provide me with competent evidence that I have any legal obligation to pay you.

Please provide me with the following:

- *Proof I agreed to this debt with my signature(s)*
- *Proof the amount you are claiming is correct and legal, which will require all statements and payment history from the original creditor*
- *Proof this account is within the Statute of Limitations and has not expired*
- *Proof you are the owner of this account, which will require the contract and terms between you and the original creditor*
- *Proof you are legally licensed (bonded and insured if applicable) to collect this debt in my state*
- *For verification purposes, I will need your business license number(s)*

If your offices have reported incorrect information to any of the three major credit bureau's (Equifax, Experian or TransUnion), said action might constitute fraud under both federal and state laws. Due to this fact, if any negative mark is found on any of my credit reports by your company or the company that you represent, I will not hesitate to bring legal action against you for the following:

- *Violation of the Fair Credit Reporting Act*
- *Violation of the Fair Debt Collection Practices Act*
- *Defamation of Character*

If your offices are able to provide the proper documentation as requested, I will require at least 30 days to investigate this information and during such time all collection activity must cease and desist.

Also during this validation period, if any action is taken which could be considered detrimental to any of my credit reports, I will consult with my legal counsel. This includes any information to a credit reporting agency that could be inaccurate or verifies that an account as accurate when in fact there is no provided proof that it is.

If your offices fail to respond to this validation request within 30 days from the date of your receipt, all references to this account must be deleted and completely removed from my credit file and a copy of such deletion request shall be sent to me immediately.

I would also like to request, in writing, that no telephone contact be made by your offices to my home or to my place of employment. If your offices attempt telephone communication with me, including but not limited to computer generated calls or correspondence sent to any third parties, it will be considered harassment, and I will have no choice but to file suit. All future communications with me MUST be done in writing and sent to the address noted in this letter.

This is an attempt to correct your records and any information obtained shall be used for that purpose.

Best Regards,

Your Signature
Your Name

What to Send Original Creditors (623 Method)

Section 623 of the Federal Credit Reporting Act gives you the right to protest items that show up on your credit report. The basic idea is that you have the right dispute your credit trade lines directly with the furnisher. You can request to see the documentation that supports the way your credit is reported. A Section 623 dispute is a dispute submitted to the original creditor.

If a record you dispute with the CRA comes back verified, you should write another dispute letter, this one to the OC referring to the dispute with the CRA, and ask the OC to conduct an INVESTIGATION. Do not ask for verification because the law calls for investigation specifically. Attach the copy of the dispute letter with the CRA or if you dispute online, furnish a dispute reference number or print out as a proof. The OC has 30 days to respond, so always use certified mail return receipt requested.

For example:

Date {MM/DD/YYYY}

Your name
Your address
City, State Zip Code
Phone/fax/email

Original Creditor name
Original Creditor address

Re: {account number}

Dear Sir or Madam,

I pulled my credit report from {Credit Reporting Agency} on {MM/DD/YYYY} only to discover that you recently have reported me 30 days late on the above account in {MM/YYYY}. I immediately disputed this information with {Credit Reporting Agency} and the results of the investigation came back Verified. First, I have never been late on this account. Second, according to the Fair Credit Reporting Act, as the information furnisher, you are required to notify me of the insertion of negative listings.

Since I have disputed the late record with the {Credit Reporting Agency}, and you verified them, I want to see what kinds of records you may have for this account. As you undoubtedly aware of, under the Fair Credit Reporting Act, you are required to conduct an investigation on this account if I request it. I therefore am submitting my written request to you to conduct such an investigation. Per the Fair Credit Reporting Act, you have 30 days to conduct this investigation and respond to my request. If you do not respond within this time period, per the Fair Credit Reporting Act, you must remove this negative information.

Sincerely,
Your signature

99 Quick Credit Tips to Keep a Perfect Credit Score!

Now that you know how to get your report and how to clean it up, you need to know how to heal your credit in general. These tips will help you improve your credit, keep your score high, and protect yourself from fraud.

1. Only apply for credit when you absolutely need it. I don't care that you can save 10% by opening a store card!

2. Order your free credit report every four months from www.annualcreditreport.com. Make sure you only get one of each credit report. For example, in January you get your Equifax report, in May get TransUnion, and in September get Experian.

3. Paying down or paying off your debt (that's reported on your credit report) will improve your score.

4. Pay on time, all the time, without fail.

5. Pay credit card balances in full each billing cycle, and if you cannot, you should maintain a balance less than or equal to 30% of your credit limit.

6. Every six months request a credit limit increase on your credit cards.

7. Never cancel your credit cards.

8. If you know you're going to be more than 30 days late paying a bill, call the creditor and ask them to give you a few more days to pay it and to not report it to the credit bureau.

9. Avoid collections!

10. If you have an account in collections, you should try to negotiate a pay for deletion before agreeing to pay the debt off.

11. Always dispute errors on your credit report. Even small ones.

12. When contacting debt collectors, always do it in writing, via certified mail with a return receipt requested.

13. To avoid missing a payment you can set up your bills for automatic payment from your checking account.

14. Maintain a bill payment calendar and check it regularly. You should even set alerts on your phone.

15. Add missing accounts to your credit report. For example, if you have a credit card that you're paying on time that's missing from the credit report, dispute it with the credit bureau to get it added.

16. Pay your credit balances before the statement comes out.

17. Mix your credit types (installment, revolving).

18. If you can't get an unsecured credit card, get a secured credit card.

19. Watch for excessive inquires on your credit report. This means both inquires that you initiated or possible fraud from identity thieves. Either way, the more inquires you have, the lower your credit score will be.

20. Add a note to your credit report if you cannot resolve a problem. For example, if a contractor refused to complete a job, and you refused to pay, you may want to note that.

21. Contact BOTH the creditors and the credit reporting agency when correcting errors.

22. Follow up on closed accounts. For example, you closed a store card years ago, but it still shows up as an open account. Make sure you get a written confirmation that the account is actually closed.

23. Ask lenders to waive late fees or charges. By waiving the late fee, which many credit card companies will do at least once, you avoid one more ding to your credit.

24. Arrange to pay your bills when you are away. Remember, you don't want to have a bunch of late fees affecting your credit just because you left the bills until you got back from vacation.

25. Do NOT use one credit card to pay another. If you are in this position, seek help with a nonprofit credit counselor.

26. If you think you have been the victim of identity theft, take action immediately.

27. Be careful where you get your credit reports. You are entitled to your free credit report from each reporting agencies. However, beware of some of the online companies that try to upsell you a "credit repair" program.

28. Give it some time. Keep in mind that most small changes you make will take some time to affect all three of your credit scores.

29. Be wary of co-signing for a loan. If you co-sign and the other party doesn't pay, you are on the hook for that debt.

30. Beware of credit repair companies and scams. Sometimes doing it yourself is the best way to repair your credit. Anyone who says, "We can erase your bad credit, 100% guaranteed!" is a liar! If you need help, you may be better off contacting a non-profit credit counseling service.

31. Live within your means. This is probably the best way to build your credit over time.

32. Where's the money? Start keeping track of the money you spend, especially all those times you whip out your credit card.

33. Avoid chasing credit card interest rate offers. "Switch now and save!" Yes, maybe, but in many cases any savings in interest rates may be offset by a reduced credit score.

34. Get your finances organized. You are less likely to miss a payment if you organize your bills and set up a regular time and place to pay them.

35. Consider simplifying your bills so that you won't forget them. For example, if you can get a bundled service plan for your TV and internet and possibly phone, you have reduced three bills down to one.

36. Stay away from payday or cash advance loans. These loans have ridiculous interest rates especially if you end up rolling over your loan until the next payday. A payday loan cycle is not a place you want to be.

37. Know your credit score before you go loan shopping. If you know your credit score, you're less likely to get cheated on financing.

38. Credit unions generally have cheaper financing than banks, especially for automobile financing. Never go with dealer financing unless you're getting an amazing deal.

39. Read the fine print on all loan agreements. I know it's not fun to read, but that's how you can differentiate one credit card offer from the next.

40. Banks often send tons of offers in the mail, to prevent yourself from falling victim to the "too good to be true deals" and the identity theft (stolen mail) make sure you opt-out of pre-screen offers.

41. Avoid overspending on sign up bonuses. They aren't free, and if you don't pay the amount in full, you could be hit with interest penalties that would cancel out any benefit of the sign up bonus.

42. Avoid signing up for business cards with your social security number. If you sign up with your social security number, you will be liable personally, not the business.

43. Your credit cards affect your credit score more than anything else on your credit report.

44. If you are getting a new loan, try to put down a larger deposit so your total loan amount is smaller.

45. You're entitled to a free credit report if a company takes "adverse action" against you, like denying your application for credit, insurance, or employment. You have to ask for your report within 60 days of receiving notice of the action.

46. It doesn't cost anything to dispute mistakes or outdated items on your credit report. Both the consumer reporting company and the information provider (the person, company, or organization that provides information about you to a consumer reporting company) are responsible for correcting inaccurate or incomplete information in your report.

47. Many states also have laws regulating credit repair companies. If you have a problem with a credit repair company, report it to your local consumer affairs office or to your state attorney general (AG).

48. If you're not disciplined enough to create a budget and stick to it, to work out a repayment plan with your creditors, or to keep track of your mounting bills, you might consider contacting a credit counseling organization. Many are nonprofit and work with you to solve your financial problems. Still, you want to remember that "nonprofit" status doesn't guarantee free, affordable, or even legitimate services.

49. If you're thinking about filing for bankruptcy, be aware that bankruptcy laws require that you get credit counseling from a government-approved organization within six months before you file for bankruptcy relief.

50. You can find a state-by-state list of government-approved organizations at www.usdoj.gov/ust, the website of the U.S. Trustee Program.

51. Be wary of credit counseling organizations that say they are government-approved but don't appear on the list of approved organizations.

52. To order your free annual report from one or all the national credit reporting companies, and to purchase your credit score, visit www.annualcreditreport.com, call toll-free 877-322-8228, or complete the Annual Credit Report Request Form and mail it to: Annual Credit Report Request Service, P. O. Box 105281, Atlanta, GA 30348-5281.

53. Your credit card company can't charge you inactivity fees, such as fees for not using your card.

54. Your credit card company can't charge you more than one fee for a single event or transaction that violates your cardholder agreement. For example, you cannot be charged more than one fee for a single late payment.

55. If your credit card company increases your card's Annual Percentage Rate (APR), it must tell you why.

56. Credit cards issued primarily for business or commercial purposes generally are not governed by the consumer protections in the Truth in Lending Act or the amendments to that act in the Credit Card Accountability, Responsibility, and Disclosure Act of 2009.

57. If your credit card is lost, stolen, or used without your authorization, you do not have to pay for any unauthorized charges greater than $50.

58. Call your credit card company as soon as you know you've lost your card or that your card number has been used without your authorization.

59. The federal government's National Do Not Call Registry is a free, easy way to reduce the telemarketing calls you get at home. To register your phone number or to get information about the registry, visit www.donotcall.gov, or call 1-888-382-1222 from the phone number you want to register. You will get fewer telemarketing calls within 31 days of registering your number. Telephone numbers on the registry will only be removed when they are disconnected and reassigned, or when you choose to remove a number from the registry.

60. If you decide that you don't want to receive prescreened offers of credit and insurance, you have two choices. You can opt out of receiving them for five years or opt out of receiving them permanently.

61. To opt out for five years, call toll-free 1-888-5-OPT-OUT (1-888-567-8688) or visit www.optoutprescreen.com. The phone number and website are operated by the major consumer reporting companies.

62. To opt out permanently you may begin the permanent Opt-Out process online at www.optoutprescreen.com. To complete your request, you must return the signed Permanent Opt-Out Election form, which will be provided after you initiate your online request.

63. The Direct Marketing Association's (DMA) Mail Preference Service (MPS) lets you opt out of receiving unsolicited commercial mail from many national companies for five years. When you register with this service, your name will be put on a "delete" file and made available to direct-mail marketers and organizations. This will reduce most of your unsolicited mail. However, your registration will not stop mailings from organizations that do not use the DMA's Mail Preference Service. To register with DMA's Mail Preference Service, go to www.dmachoice.org

64. The DMA also has an Email Preference Service (eMPS) to help you reduce unsolicited commercial emails. To opt out of receiving unsolicited commercial email from DMA members, visit www.dmachoice.org. Registration is free and good for six years.

65. If you think you may have been scammed, file a complaint with the Federal Trade Commission. If you are outside the U.S., file a complaint at www.econsumer.gov. Visit ftc.gov/idtheft, where you'll find out how to minimize your risk of identity theft. Report scams to your state attorney general.

66. A debt collector may not contact you at inconvenient times or places, such as before 8 a.m. or after 9 p.m., unless you agree to it. Collectors may not contact you at work if they're told (orally or in writing) that you're not allowed to get calls there.

67. Every collector must send you a written "validation notice" telling you how much money you owe within five days after they first contact you. This notice also must include the name of the creditor to whom you owe the money, and how to proceed if you don't think you owe the money.

68. If you send the debt collector a letter stating that you don't owe any or all of the money, or asking for verification of the debt, that collector must stop contacting you. You have to send that letter within 30 days after you receive the validation notice. However, a collector can begin contacting you again if it sends you written verification of the debt, like a copy of a bill for the amount you owe.

69. Debt collectors may not harass, oppress, or abuse you. They can't do the following: use threats of violence or harm, publish a list of names of people who refuse to pay their debts (but they can give this information to the credit reporting companies), use obscene or profane language, or repeatedly use the phone to annoy someone.

70. Debt collectors may not lie when they are trying to collect a debt.

71. Debt collectors also are prohibited from saying that you will be arrested if you don't pay your debt, that they'll seize, garnish, attach, or sell your property or wages unless they are permitted

by law to take the action and intend to do so, or that legal action will be taken against you, if doing so would be illegal or if they don't intend to take the action.

72. Debt collectors may not give false credit information about you to anyone, including a credit reporting company, send you anything that looks like an official document from a court or government agency if it isn't, or use a false company name.

73. Debt collectors may not engage in unfair practices when they try to collect a debt. For example, they may not try to collect any interest, fee, or other charge on top of the amount you owe unless the contract that created your debt—or your state law—allows the charge. They may not deposit a post-dated check early, take or threaten to take your property unless it can be done legally, or contact you by postcard.

74. If a debt collector is trying to collect more than one debt from you, the collector must apply any payment you make to the debt you select. Equally important, a debt collector may not apply a payment to a debt you don't think you owe.

75. If you don't pay a debt, a creditor or its debt collector generally can sue you to collect. If they win, the court will enter a judgment against you. The judgment states the amount of money you owe and allows the creditor or collector to get a garnishment order against you, directing a third party, like your bank, to turn over funds from your account to pay the debt.

76. Federal benefits, such as the following, are exempt from garnishment:

- Social Security Benefits
- Supplemental Security Income (SSI) Benefits
- Veterans' Benefits
- Civil Service and Federal Retirement and Disability Benefits
- Service Members' Pay
- Military Annuities and Survivors' Benefits
- Student Assistance
- Railroad Retirement Benefits
- Merchant Seamen Wages
- Longshoremen's and Harbor Workers' Death and Disability Benefits
- Foreign Service Retirement and Disability Benefits
- Compensation for Injury, Death, or Detention of Employees of U.S. Contractors Outside the U.S.
- Federal Emergency Management Agency Federal Disaster Assistance

77. If the collector does something illegal, you have the right to sue the collector in a state or federal court within one year from the date on which they violated a law. If you win, the judge

can require the collector to pay you for any damages you can prove you suffered because of the illegal collection practices, like lost wages and medical bills. The judge can require the debt collector to pay you up to $1,000, even if you can't prove that you suffered actual damages. You also can be reimbursed for your attorney's fees and court costs.

78. If a debt collector files a lawsuit against you to collect a debt, you need to respond to the lawsuit, either personally or through your lawyer, by the date specified in the court papers in order to preserve your rights.

79. Report any problems you have with a debt collector to your state attorney general's office (naag.org) and the Federal Trade Commission (ftc.gov). Many states have their own debt collection laws that are different from the federal Fair Debt Collection Practices Act. Your attorney general's office can help you determine your rights under your state's law.

80. If you have old debts, collectors may not be able to sue you to collect on them. That's because debt collectors have a limited number of years—known as the statute of limitations—to sue you to collect. After that, your unpaid debts are considered "time-barred." According to the law, a debt collector cannot sue you for not paying a debt that's time-barred.

81. If you're sued to collect on a time-barred debt, pay attention, and respond. Consider talking to an attorney. You or your attorney should tell the judge that the debt is time-barred and, as proof, provide a copy of the verification from the collector or any information you have that shows the date of your last payment. The lawsuit will be dismissed if the judge decides the debt is time-barred. In any case, don't ignore the lawsuit. If you do, the collector likely will get a court judgment against you, and possibly take money from your paycheck, bank account, or tax refund.

82. Family members typically are not obligated to pay the debts of a deceased relative from their own assets.

83. Debt settlement programs often ask—or encourage—you to stop sending payments directly to your creditors, and this may have a negative impact on your credit report and other consequences. For example, your debts may continue to accrue late fees and penalties that can put you further in the hole. You also may get calls from your creditors or debt collectors requesting repayment. You could even be sued for repayment.

84. Avoid doing business with any company that promises to settle your debt if the company:

- Charges any fees before it settles your debts
- Touts a "new government program" to bail out personal credit card debt
- Guarantees it can make your unsecured debt go away

- Tells you to stop communicating with your creditors but doesn't explain the serious consequences
- Tells you it can stop all debt collection calls and lawsuits
- Guarantees that your unsecured debts can be paid off for pennies on the dollar

85. Before you enroll in a debt settlement program, do your homework. You're making a big decision that involves spending a lot of your money—money that could go toward paying down your debt. Check out the company with your State attorney general and local consumer protection agency. They can tell you if any consumer complaints are on file about the firm you're considering. Ask your state attorney general if the company is required to be licensed to work in your state.

86. If you do business with a debt settlement company, you may have to put money in a dedicated bank account, which will be administered by an independent third party. The funds are yours, and you are entitled to the interest that accrues. The account administrator may charge you a reasonable fee for account maintenance and is responsible for transferring funds from your account to pay your creditors and the debt settlement company when settlements occur.

87. Before you sign up for the service, the debt relief company must give you information about the program:

- The price and terms: The company must explain its fees and any conditions on its services.
- The company must tell you how long it will take to get results: They must tell you how many months or years before it will make an offer to each creditor for a settlement.
- Offers: The company must tell you how much money or the percentage of each outstanding debt you must save before it will make an offer to each creditor on your behalf.
- Non-payment: If the company asks you to stop making payments to your creditors—or if the program relies on you to not make payments—it must tell you about the possible negative consequences of your actions, including damage to your credit report and credit score. They must tell you that if you stop paying, your creditors may sue you or continue with the collections process and that your credit card companies may charge you additional fees and interest, which will increase the amount you owe.

88. The debt relief company also must tell you that:

- The funds are yours, and you are entitled to the interest earned.
- The account administrator is not affiliated with the debt relief provider and doesn't get referral fees.
- You may withdraw your money any time without penalty.

89. Depending on your financial condition, any savings you get from debt relief services can be considered income and taxable.

90. Credit card companies and others may report settled debt to the IRS, which the IRS considers income, unless you are "insolvent."

91. Insolvency is when your total debts are more than the fair market value of your total assets. Insolvency can be complex to determine.

92. Most reputable credit counselors are non-profits and offer services through local offices, online, or on the phone. If possible, find an organization that offers in-person counseling. Many universities, military bases, credit unions, housing authorities, and branches of the U.S. Cooperative Extension Service operate non-profit credit counseling programs.

93. Credit card issuers must include a toll-free number on their statements that gives cardholders information about finding non-profit counseling organizations.

94. Declaring bankruptcy has serious consequences, including lowering your credit score.

95. Filing for bankruptcy under Chapter 13 allows people with a steady income to keep property, like a mortgaged house or a car that they might otherwise lose through the Chapter 7 bankruptcy process.

96. In Chapter 13, the court approves a repayment plan that allows you to pay off your debts over three to five years, without surrendering any property. After you have made all the payments under the plan, your debts are discharged.

97. Set up a budget and live within it. Credit should not be used to live beyond your means. By setting a budget and living within it, you will avoid overextending your credit.

98. Shred everything. One of the ways that would-be identity thieves acquire information is through "dumpster-diving," aka trash-picking. If you are throwing out bills and credit card statements, old credit card or ATM receipts, medical statements or even junk-mail solicitations for credit cards and mortgages, you may be leaving too much information lying around. Buy a personal shredder and shred all papers with personally identifiable information on them before disposing of them.

99. The only place to get your real credit score is myFICO.com

7 Credit Card Myths—Busted!

Who hasn't caught an episode of *MythBusters* on the Discovery Channel? It's an entertaining production focused on debunking urban myths in a tongue-in-cheek style. Myths arise about many of life's experiences and that includes the ubiquitous credit card. Today, we will look at seven common myths regarding credit cards, and then we'll debunk them.

Separating Fact from Fiction

Myth # 1—My credit card has no limit.

No such thing! Every credit card has a limit. Your card issuer just doesn't reveal what that limit is. This gives you the illusion of being special. Sooner or later, you will bump up against that limit. I can only hope it doesn't happen when you are picking up the tab for dinner with your boss...

Myth # 2—Opening a new credit card will lower my credit score.

Actually, it may help! Credit scores, in part, are based on credit utilization. Just opening a new credit card increases the overall amount of credit available to you. If you don't use the card, this has the effect of reducing the percentage of utilization, which ***helps*** your credit score.

Myth # 3—Refusing a credit limit increase will damage my credit score.

It just ain't so! Credit card issuers like to make more credit available to good customers and the offer is a compliment. Declining to accept the offer is of zero consequence to your credit score. Not to get too far into the weeds here, but a limit increase reduces your percentage of utilization, and that *is* a positive thing for your credit score ... provided you don't use all of the additional available credit.

Myth # 4—Canceling some of my credit cards will improve my credit score.

Where did this come from!? Again, we are talking about credit utilization ratios. Canceling cards reduces your available credit relative to your existing balances. This raises your credit utilization percentage which damages your credit score. Don't do it!

Myth # 5—My limit is "X" ... so I must be able to afford it.

Credit card issuers have no crystal ball and no moral imperative to look out for your best interests. Credit limits are set based on scores, debt-to-income ratios and other factors. By simply granting a limit of "X" the credit card issuer is not making the assertion that you can afford it. While it is true that they try to establish limits leading to favorable repayment outcomes, they don't know you, and they cannot foresee what financial crises may pop up in your life.

Myth # 6—I'm pre-approved for this card ... so I am guaranteed to receive it.

Really? I don't think so! This is a marketing ploy and often a cruel one. Pre-approved should be changed to read pre-screened. All that means is that you have been selected as a likely candidate to *apply* for the credit card. You will still need to meet the credit standards of the card issuer before you ever swipe that plastic.

Myth # 7—Entering my PIN backwards at the ATM alerts the "popo" to a robbery.

No clue how this got started, but it is patently false. Think about it ... people have PINs such as 7007, 1111 and other numerical palindromes. If this myth were true, these people would all be behind bars for falsely reporting a crime ... duh!

This Has Been Fun...

So here are three more myths, just for grins.

Bonus Myth # 1—Pre-paid and debit cards help my credit score

If it were only true! But it isn't. Pre-paid card issuers do not report to the credit reporting agencies, and why should they? You are spending your own money, not borrowed money. The same is true with debit cards.

Bonus Myth # 2—You shouldn't borrow from one card to pay another

Robbing Peter to pay Paul is not always a bad thing. If you find yourself in a temporary financial squeeze, it is okay to borrow from another card to make the payment. Skipping a payment or being late on a payment can really hurt your credit score. Isn't a balance transfer the same as using one card to pay another? We do that all the time! Still if you find yourself in this situation more than once, you should consider contacting a credit counseling service.

Bonus Myth # 3—There is nothing wrong with making the minimum payment

Yes ...and no! It's okay if you are in a bind and can't pay more, but it should *not* be something that you practice regularly. Paying only the minimum will barely cover the interest on the account and principal reductions are tiny!

Warning! Are You Making These 5 Credit Repair Mistakes

You usually have the choice when it comes to repairing your credit. You can actually do it yourself, or you can hire a professional. If you do it yourself, you have double check everything that you do so that you don't make an error. If you hire a professional, you also have to check their work. A professional is just another human being, after all, and can fall prey to mistakes.

When it comes to repairing your bad credit and raising your credit score, there are a number of things that you can do. It can be tricky to navigate through this process, so you should watch out for the wrong ways to fix your credit. Not only do these things have the potential to cause even more damage, they can make it even harder to proceed with credit repair once you have made those mistakes.

1. Shortening Your Credit History

It can be difficult to manage several credit cards. You get panicky at the thought of the due date because you have to pay all of them at the same time. Sometimes, people close a credit card once they pay off a big balance. This is done to remove the temptation of having a credit card that has some unused credit. However, this can be a wrong move. One of the computations used to calculate your credit score is the amount of credit that you have used versus the totality of your credit limit. This is called the utilization ratio. Once you close out a card, you take that credit limit out the equation, thereby increasing your credit utilization ratio. Removing a card also removes it from your credit history. If it is one of your older cards, closing it can shorten your payment history, which is a major component of your credit score.

2. Consolidating Debt

Credit card companies have all these promotions to entice people to sign up. One such promo is a lower interest rate when transferring your debt from another card to this new one. Sometimes, you can transfer several balances so that you will only have to make a single payment every month. Consolidating is actually a bad idea because it is not a real solution to your debt problem. You are just transferring your credit and not working towards paying for it. The debt still exists. Moreover, if your bad habits still remain unchanged, it might be tempting for you to use those cards that now have credit. If you do that, you will just end up adding to your debt.

3. Debt Financing

Debt financing refers to the practice of applying for a loan to pay off more urgent loans and credit card bills. That gives you more breathing room because it gives you more time to find ways to pay off your debt.

One of the most common examples is a college student applying for a student loan and using the money to make car payments or pay off a credit card that has been used to go on a shopping spree. Debt financing is a really bad way to repair your credit. You don't really make any inroads into paying off your debt. In fact, you even pile more debt because you end up paying for two interest rates, the one on your first loan and the one on your current loan. You'll just end up owing money for an even longer period of time.

4. Living Without Credit

After years of scrambling to make those credit card or loan payments, you are finally at a point where you can live debt free. In fact, you now have savings in the bank. This is a very good thing. However, you might have the impulse to close out your accounts or not use any credit at all. This can be harmful to you in the event you might need to make any kind of loan in the future, such a business loan for your start up company. Banks will take a look at your credit history and they may deny your loan application if you don't have any recent credit history. It is better to keep you credit accounts open and use then a similar manner to your debit card. Charge purchases so that your credit history moves, but you want to pay off the entire balance each month so that your debt does not pile up once more.

5.   No Documentation

Always document your credit repair process. This is recommended so that you will be able to track your progress against a checklist of certain tasks that you need to accomplish during the credit repair process. Proper documentation can also be your biggest tool when you have to dispute items on your credit report. Documentation establishes credibility and authenticity, and it is the best way to state your case.

Don't Do It! Put That Debit Card Away

Stop! Don't Do It! Madam, please step away from that terminal.

At least, not until you know the facts–the real facts about your debit card and how using your debit card may be costing you more than you think.

Debit Cards

Look, it's absolutely true, debit cards can be a great convenience. Really, debit cards are easy to use, you don't have to worry about carrying extra cash or hunting for an ATM machine (do people still do that?). You also don't have to pay those ridiculous credit card interest charges or fees.

Still, there is another side to debit card use, and this is definitely a case of what you don't know can hurt you.

Here's what this is all about. Debit cards are NOT credit cards. Nope, not today, not tomorrow. Sure, your debit card *looks* like a credit card. Sure, your debit feels like a credit card, and it probably even has the Master Card or Visa Card logo just like a real credit card too.

Facts about Debit Cards You May Not Know

Yet, what's hidden behind this facade?

Number 1 - This can be HUGE! Your debit card is directly linked to your checking account. Do you get the point here? I mean really? Once again, your debit card is linked DIRECTLY TO YOUR CHECKING ACCOUNT! What does this mean? Hello! Can you say bye bye to your money?

If you get suckered into a fraudulent transaction, the money is gone before you know it. Yes, it's true there is a federal law to protect you against fraudulent activity, but you only have two days to notify your bank of the fraudulent transaction. If you don't realize your debit card has been stolen or compromised, your potential liability increases up to $500.00 or even more depending on the circumstances. You know how friendly the bank customer service staff is nowadays. Hope you weren't planning on renting a car to get home since there's no more money in the bank account.

Ouch! Oh, and by the way, remember the money is already gone from bank account. This reason alone is why so many financial consumer advocates encourage extreme vigilance or even avoidance with your debit card usage.

Number 2 - Dispute rights … or more specifically, the lack thereof. What does this mean? A credit card offers dispute rights that most debit cards do not. As you probably know, when you use a *"real"* credit card to make a purchase, you have what is referred to as an "added layer of protection." The credit card issuers often help mediate or resolve disputes, even though they prefer you deal with the merchants first.

Your debit card issuing bank, uh, not so much. No such added protection. Sure, you can report a fraudulent transaction. Sure, you have limited liability (subject to reporting requirements, etc.), but as far as your bank helping resolve a dispute between you and a merchant? Don't hold your breath.

Number 3 - Overdrawn bank accounts! Ouch! This one can get pretty painful. Here's what happens. So, let's say you are in the toy store with your 3 year old. You give in to her and end up buying her another little doll, using your debit card. You are confident its okay to use the debit card because you are almost positive you know how much is in the account. So, the transaction is approved and you and little Sara head home.

Oops, not so fast there big fellow. Unbeknownst to you, at the same time, your wife was grocery shopping at the supermarket, knowing there is a big gathering this Sunday, she really stocked up on groceries. I mean really stocked up, like to the tune of a couple of hundred bucks. Uh Oh! Guess what, both transactions were approved, but now your checking account is overdrawn. Oh sure, your bank went ahead and authorized the transaction. I mean you did sign that little disclosure document a few months ago about approving debit card transactions. Remember that one, the disclosure in 2-point type that neither you nor wife could figure out, but signed anyway?

I mean it sounded right, *"Doesn't everyone want their debit card transactions approved?"* So now you are in the hole, so to speak, and it may be a day or so before you figure out that your checking account isn't as full as you thought, buy don't worry, the bank has authorized your transaction, simply charging a little fee in exchange.

Good grief, does this mean you should never use your debit card? Of course not, but if you choose to use a debit card, you must know the facts.

You Will Never Get the Best Rates on Your Credit Cards! Suckers!

You have certainly seen the ads on TV or gotten the piles of junk mail with terrific sounding super low interest rate credit cards. You may have also noticed that the credit cards companies are at it again as the economy starts making some progress towards improvement, but do you know the real story behind these super low interest offers? The truth about teaser credit card rates may surprise you.

Are There Rules about Credit Card Offers?

Certainly! Here in the United States, credit card offers are governed by the Federal Trade Commission in addition to other federal agencies. The bottom line is that advertisements cannot be deceptive or misleading. However, your interpretation of deceptive or misleading may be pretty far off what actually happens with credit card offers.

Credit Card Company Offers and You

The reality with low-rate or zero interest loan offers is that the advertised rate and offer must be available. But here's the catch—they don't have to make the lowest rate available to everyone that applies. The credit card companies refer to these as representative rates. Have you read the fine print on those offers? Somewhere in the extremely fine print that you just about need a microscope to read will be the real conditions. You may be surprised to learn about the real limitations and qualifications necessary to get the advertised rate.

Consider this real world example. There is a retired gentleman who owns a $1 million dollar home plus a second home in another country. He is a retired corporate executive, and he is current on all his loans and has significant equity in both homes. Yet, even he was just recently denied the best rate even though his credit score was near perfect.

The Rest of the Story, What Happened, and Why

Why was the gentleman above given a higher rate than advertised by his own bank? As discussed above, remember that advertised rates are "representative rates." Per credit industry guidelines, representative rates are not guaranteed to all applicants. To avoid being deceptive and misleading, the low rates have to be real and available to a certain number of applicants. However, that might mean you don't make the cut.

Factors that Affect Your Getting the Best Rate

First, consider where you are applying. Banking representatives have admitted that they give the best rates to their own customers. Yet even that may not be enough. Even if you apply to your local bank where you have had a banking relationship for years, your application may still fall short. Keep in mind your bank can pull up all of your banking history. Any overdrafts or long periods of low balances may weigh against you when applying for the best rate.

Take a look at this typical scenario. A customer of a local bank applies for a low interest credit card offer from her bank. This customer has enjoyed a nine year relationship with this bank, has never made a late payment and feels she is a "shoe-in" to get the best rate. Oops, not so fast. Look there, she opens her mailbox and finds a shiny new credit card. However, as she reads the terms of her new card she realizes her rate is two percentage points higher than the advertised rate. Puzzled, she grabs her cell phone and calls the 1-800 phone number to find out why. After wading through the phone tree menu, she finally gets through. She asks why her rate is higher than the advertised rate. The customer service person on the other end patiently explains that she got the higher rate because of the total amount of debt she was still carrying plus the two overdrafts she had on her personal checking account.

Do You Stand a Chance?

From the two examples discussed above that it may seem hopeless. It may look like there is nothing you can do. Perhaps you will get the best rate. Then again, maybe you won't. But, actually there are two things you will want to consider in order to keep in mind to maximize your chances of getting the best rate. You will want to consider these factors before you just wildly apply for those low rate offers. Remember, more is not better. Too many applications for credit really will lower your credit score which will almost certainly mean you will not get the best rate.

First, you will want a clean credit report with no late payments, a relatively low amount of debt, etc. Second, as pointed out by banking loan officers, sometimes you will stand a better chance if you respond to an offer with your local bank, assuming you have a good relationship with them. Also, if you are working with your local bank, you may find it helpful to visit your branch manager in person.

Getting the best cad card interest can seem like you are playing the lottery. In many cases, the exact criteria that lenders use to award the best interest rates are not revealed. Nevertheless, there are some things you to be aware of to increase your chances of getting that low rate.

Tales from the Darkside: Credit Error Horror Story

You have probably heard about how crucial it is for you to know your own personal credit details, such as your credit score and the contents of your credit report, and to take quick action if you see something that doesn't look right. Still, have you seriously considered how valuable knowing about your credit actually is? Look at this true story about a mother in California.

Her Story, Victim or Hero?

Heather Rose had finally had it with credit card turndowns. She had been applying for new credit cards but kept getting turned down. She thought she was a good candidate for a new credit card and was puzzled by the rejection notices she kept receiving in the mail.

Finally, she did what any responsible consumer knows to do. She called and asked for her credit report. Upon receiving her report credit, she spotted the problem immediately, a whopping

$16,159 single judgment against her, but there was a big problem here. Her credit report showed a court judgment from Chase Bank. The judgment, for $16,159 was for a credit card she had never even possessed, much less used. "What's wrong with this picture?" she thought to herself.

So Heather did the next thing responsible consumers have been taught, she contacted two of the leading three credit reporting agencies. She attempted to correct the matter directly with TransUnion and Equifax. Unfortunately for her, she could not get the issue resolved with either one of these two credit reporting agencies.

Undeterred, Heather took the next logical step. Heather contacted Chase Bank directly. Surely, the bank that issued the credit card can research this and clear my record she must have been thinking. Well, not so much. According to Heather, Chase Bank refused to deal with her at all.

"Oh no you don't," Heather said to herself and promptly contacted her local media. Amazingly, within a remarkably short time, Chase Bank sent Heather a letter indicating there was no judgment against her after all. Soon thereafter, her credit reports were cleared up with TransUnion and Equifax.

Lessons from Heather's Experience

1. Know your Number

Ignorance may be bliss, but it could murder your credit score. In Heather's case, she stated that she was puzzled by rejections for new credit. However, as you see here, once Heather laid her hands on her own credit report, she found the problem remarkably quickly and corrected this problem, (albeit with some extreme measures). The lesson for you is to know your number! Check your credit report frequently. As you probably know, you are entitled to one free credit report each year. You can also stagger your credit reports so that you get a fresh credit report every four months by using a different credit reporting agency. Go back to Heather's tale above. Can you see how much easier it would have been for Heather had she been regularly checking her credit report?

2. Know Where to Go for Help

Now, you probably will not end up calling your local television consumer help line, but there are avenues for you to get help. In Heather's case, she did some things exactly right. She checked her credit report for errors. Once she found a very large error, Heather attempted the most obvious method, she contacted the credit reporting agencies directly. When that didn't work, she contacted the credit card issuing bank directly. The next step (setting aside your local media as a realistic option) would be to contact a new federal agency created in 2010 called the Consumer Financial Protection Bureau (CFPB), this agency is setup for situations just like the one described here. Specifically, the CFPB was set up as another consumer protection agency, to protect you against predatory lending, misleading banking policies, etc. They are on the web at: http://www.consumerfinance.gov/. There you will find a direct online portal to submit a complaint directly.

3. Don't Give Up

Heather Rose's tale is a very good case history that illustrates the importance of persistence is in fixing your credit report errors. Much like the Energizer Bunny she just kept going and going, until the error on her credit report was fixed.

Your credit report is a tool used by both potential lenders and you. You owe it to yourself to know about your credit report and how to fix errors that might show up unexpectedly.

New Credit Rules: Rent Payments will Affect Your Credits Score!

You need to know that there have been significant changes in the credit-reporting arena and provisions of the Credit Card Act of 2009, which recently took effect and may affect you in a major way.

Retired, Widowed or Divorced

Effective October 11th, 2011, a provision of the CARD Act of 2009 became enforceable and will severely impact a significant number of consumers. Credit card companies are now required to consider an applicant's independent ability to make payments with no regard to age. That means that homemakers, non-working college students, widows, divorcees and others in similar circumstances can no longer qualify for a credit card in their name. Richard Cordray, Director of the CFPB, in testimony before the House Financial Services Committee, acknowledged that this was an unintended consequence and assured the committee that it will be corrected by way of the agency's rule-making authority. It has not happened yet, but watch for it!

A New Watchdog

This change is going to affect you indirectly, but it will affect you. As of September 30, 2012, there is a new cop on the beat. The Consumer Financial Protection Bureau, established to oversee credit-reporting agencies and monitor their business practices, conduct on-site investigations, and craft new rules with regard to their operations. Credit reporting agencies have significant power over each of our lives, and it is high time they get the regulatory attention they deserve.

Best Pay the Rent on Time

Up to now, about the only way rental payments found its way into a credit report were if the property owner won a judgment for back rent. This is not the case any longer. Experian has pioneered a unit they call "RentBureau" which tracks the payment record of renters as reported by member property owners. Experian is including this information on its credit reports. This could be a plus for those with limited credit histories, and it will be an invaluable aid to property owners as a means of pressuring tenants to pay on time or pay the consequences on their credit history. How this will factor into your overall credit score is uncertain. Rest assured, TransUnion and Equifax will be introducing its version soon. Competition demands it! If you have been a pain in your landlord's posterior, let the schmoozing begin!

Payday Loans, Debt Settlements and Rent to Own

These "shadow" credit transactions have largely been outside the scope of the big-three credit reporting agencies. However, just this year FICO developed an enhanced credit score in conjunction with its partner, CoreLogic, which they call the FICO Mortgage Score. By all accounts, this score was developed to provide lenders with a better tool for evaluating credit risk in the wake of the subprime mortgage crisis. This casts a wider net than the traditional FICO score and can include payday loans, rent-to-own agreements, and other credit transactions that are typically under the radar. As with all new developments, this one has pros and cons. Capturing this previously undisclosed credit information could be a plus for those seeking credit, particularly a mortgage, but have a sparse amount of conventional credit. Having payday loan obligations that were paid according to terms, rent-to-own, and other previously, "shadow" agreements, become part of a credit file would be a positive development with the potential to put conventional credit within the grasp of a wider pool of applicants. However, this may unfairly demonize consumers with legitimate disputes that have withheld payment for good cause.

Expanded Role

The Consumer Financial Protection Bureau is going to have a full plate as it struggles to monitor and regulate the ever-expanding scope of the credit reporting agencies. We will all have to keep our collective ear to the ground in an effort to keep pace with the inevitable changes that come about as new products come to the fore and the regulators try to regulate them. At least we can be grateful this agency is in place.

Your Credit Score May Be Wrong Because of This

You already know how terribly valuable your credit report and your credit score are in today's society. However, contrary to what you may have been told, actually correcting errors or omissions on your credit report is not a simple or a straightforward task.

Ignoring Consumer Requests?

According to the Consumer Financial Protection Bureau (CFPB), some if not all, of the credit reporting agencies aren't so quick to move when you provide documentation. The CFPB report makes the case that oftentimes, the credit reporting agencies actually ignore consumer supplied evidence. Typically, it starts when a consumer sees an erroneous item on his credit report. As a responsible consumer, he promptly notifies all three credit reporting agencies. However, this is where the process starts to break down. Once he sends in his supporting documentation, this evidence never makes it to anyone who can correct the issue.

What's Going On?

The answer might not surprise you, and it's all about the automation of the credit dispute process. You see, the big three credit reporting agencies have all switched to an automated credit dispute system. Here's how the system currently works:

- You find an error on your credit report.

- You notify all three credit reporting agencies.

- The credit reporting agency representatives (if you actually speak to someone on the phone) or the online process directs you to send in your documentation.

- Your credit dispute is given a code. Your individual credit dispute code tells the automated system how to classify this dispute this is and where the information needs to go.

- Your evidence arrives, but from there, no one is quite sure what happens. Your evidence is supposed to go directly to the data furnishers. Data furnishers simply are the financial institutions that supply the credit reporting agencies with their data. Currently, these data furnishers are responsible for about 85% of credit dispute assessments.

- However, here is where the problem shows up. According to the Consumer Financial Protection Bureau (CFPB), this evidence rarely, if ever, gets forwarded to the data furnishers. You might be asking yourself—if your evidence does not get sent to the data furnishers, where does it actually go? Unfortunately, for now, the answer is unclear, almost like a credit dispute black hole. No wonder they tell you not to send in the originals, and you are instructed to make copies.

What's Wrong with the Process?

The short answer is simply this: complete automation. That is, the evidence you provide gets little if any live interaction with a real human being. To put it another way, this means that the current system apparently does not even have a person in charge of looking at evidence provided by consumers.

The longer answer could be serious, some might actually consider it a violation of federal law. As you probably know, the Fair Credit and Reporting Act requires credit reporting agencies to address credit disputes within 30 days. Although the credit reporting agencies are most likely compliant with the initial assessment of your credit dispute within 30 days, they may be lurking in a gray area if they fail to forward supporting evidence or have systems in place examining the evidence you provide.

Spokespersons from CFPB have so far declined to comment on the automated credit dispute issue, responding that they are indeed looking at the issue. However, the CFPB did release the following information about examples of errors they have already found in credit reports:

- Incomplete or erroneous information provided during a loan application process
- Mismatches between consumer supplied data with file data
- Missing identifying information from government records

A Growing Trend?

As you might suspect, there is not yet a strong motivation for the credit reporting agencies to modify their systems because by using an automated processing system the credit reporting agencies are saving tons of money. Consider, perhaps the cost savings are significant enough to afford the occasional lawsuit from a disgruntled consumer.

Is there a way out of this mess if you have a credit dispute?

Actually, now there is another alternative. The CFPB has just setup an online portal where you can submit your credit dispute directly through their website. That link can be found right here: http://www.consumerfinance.gov/complaint/

Correcting errors on your credit report can be a time consuming and difficult process. The process is even more difficult if supporting evidence you carefully assemble and forward is ignored. Thankfully, there is another way, through the Consumer Financial Protection Bureau.

Fake Credit Score? How to Tell the Difference!

You already know your credit score is extremely important these days. By now, you have probably heard various terms thrown about for credit score formulas and calculations. However, you may not know that all credit scores are not the same. In a society where the right credit score can open a lot of doors for you, it is necessary for you to understand the difference between the credit score a potential lender or employer may look at, and the other credit scores out there.

Back to the Basics: Short Primer on Your Credit Score

Let's start with a good working definition for credit score. Your credit score is simply a number. This number is the result of a extraordinarily sophisticated mathematical algorithm (fancy word for a complicated set of formulas).

Here's how it works. The company calculating your credit score considers five facets of your financial life. They consider your payment history, how much you owe, how long you have had any sort of credit, the type of credit you have (revolving or installment) and finally, how many recent searches for credit show up in your files. After all of this data is fed into their algorithm, your credit score is then spit out for the entire world to see, or at least the world you have given access to your credit report.

The bottom line is that they are only trying to predict whether or not you will repay borrowed money and your credit score is used as a gauge for your creditworthiness.

Origins of the Credit Score

Your credit score is actually the creation of a company called FICO. Fair, Isaac and Company was founded way back in 1956. Shortly after the company's founding, they began selling their proprietary credit scoring system. The company has grown and is now a public company. Their proprietary credit scoring system, called FICO, has become the de facto standard for credit reporting.

The New Pretenders

Keep in mind that FICO sells their scoring system to credit reporting agencies. Not to be outdone, the credit reporting agencies began creating their own credit scores in an attempt to challenge the virtual monopoly held by FICO. These challengers to the FICO scoring model have been given the euphemistic term FAKO.

Why FAKO? Some in the credit and financial industry contend that these new competitors are fakes, thus the name FAKO. At this point, the name has stuck and most consider there to be two contenders for your credit score: FICO and FAKO.

Who Are the FAKO Players?

1. Vantage Score: Vantage Score is the result of a team effort from the big three credit reporting agencies to come up with their credit scoring model. One advantage to using Vantage Score is that it's a merged score, meaning it combines data from the big three. The disadvantage to Vantage Score is that hardly anyone uses it.

2. PLUS: Plus is a proprietary creation from Experian. Since the PLUS score is only based on internal data from Experian, it's not terribly useful to you aside from your own educational value. Also, keep in mind, the PLUS score is not used by any lenders.

3. TransRisk: Transrisk Plus is a proprietary creation from Transunion. You should not be surprised to learn that just like the PLUS score above, it's not much use beyond your own educational value.

What Should You Do?

The most noteworthy thing you should do is to know your number, your real credit score number, if you're curious. Still, reviewing your credit reports is more useful than knowing the actual number. To date, the credit score based on FICO is the credit industry standard. Most importantly, the FICO score is the score that potential lenders view. Additionally, keep in mind that your credit score is not the same as your credit report. Note that your FICO credit score number may actually be different for each credit reporting agency since your information may not be the same on each report.

The increasing use of personal credit scores has recently spawned competitors in the credit scoring market. Be smart and know your real credit score number or simply review your credit reports regularly. Don't be fooled by the FAKO's. The credit score number you want to know is the same one the lenders look at—your FICO score.

The FICO Score May Be Going the Way of the VHS

Not long ago, I raised the subject about the significance of credit scores in other aspects of our lives, and touched on the importance (right or wrong) of FICO's credit score in terms of employment, insurance rates, qualifying for an apartment and even accessing utility services. As I browsed the web the other day, I had what can only be described as a WTF moment. Hang on … much of what you have come to believe about credit scoring is on a path to change and in a dramatic way. Are you sitting down? I mean really—sit down!

We are on the cusp of having our social media interactions converted into a new credit score. Facebook, Instagram, Twitter and other social media sites, are about to be employed as a baseline for your creditworthiness. This is rumored to be based on your social circle, your interests, your hobbies and other data gathered from your social media pages. In short, a credit score tied to how your life is mirrored by social media. Like I said … WTF!

This monstrosity is dubbed "the super score" and quite frankly, I don't see anything *super* about it. Check that; I *do* find it super invasive of our privacy. All right, I understand the argument that having a social media presence is a matter of choice. I get that! No one is forced to open a Facebook account, sign up for Twitter or subscribe to Instagram. More to the point, people can and do choose what they share on these sites, who they "friend" and what they tweet.

That said, does any sane individual believe their choice of friends, what they say and what they photograph should be connected in any way, shape or form to their ability to secure a credit card, an auto loan, or a mortgage, much less insurance, a roof over their head, or a job!

What's Wrong with FICO?

This is where it really gets interesting. The FICO score has been the gold standard for the lending community for around three decades or so. As a result of the financial crisis, the reliability of the FICO score is apparently on the decline.

Andy Jennings, the chief analytics officer and head honcho of FICO Labs, says, "When the economy gets worse, risk gets worse, and when the economy gets better, risk profiles and risk levels improve. Jennings goes on to say, "One of the drawbacks of the way we model risk today is that it amplifies both cycles." Jennings points out, "As risks increase, banks' capital requirements increase when it's too late to make a difference." Jennings concludes, "You have to put capital away when times are good, not when times are bad."

The long and short of it is that the cycle Jennings refers to has confused the model. While today a credit score of 700 might equate with a 1 in 20 chance of the borrower defaulting, were the economy to get worse, the odds could rise to 1 in 15, even though the credit score is unchanged! No wonder the lenders have their knickers in a knot.

FICO is not in the business of economic forecasting, which means someone has to provide FICO with a qualified opinion about where the economy is going. Then FICO could make the adjustments necessary to resolve the problems of the model … but no one has stepped up to the plate with a forecast that everyone can agree on.

Add to That

There are now fewer potential borrowers with flawless credit records. Statistics suggest that as much as 25 percent of the adult U.S. population do not even have a credit record. This is another reason banks are looking at alternative or additional data pools to develop a scoring system.

Risk Management Technology

Apparently, risk management technology is big business, expected to approach $74 billion worldwide. Not a small chunk of change to be sure. Small wonder the geeks are working overtime to come up with new ways to satisfy the credit industry's thirst to reduce the numbers of nonperforming loans and thereby increase their profit margins. According to the *American Banker,* the level of satisfaction with current risk management technology is not high, with 72% of the banks surveyed indicating that they will increase their spending on risk avoidance technology by 15%.

With this much money at stake, the innovators are out in force. I was surprised to learn that the idea of using social media for making credit decisions was developed in the Philippines. On reflection, I can see why. Culturally, Filipinos are instinctively averse to public embarrassment and place a high value on how they are perceived by others. Given the fact that around 9 out of 10 Filipinos have a Facebook account and there are no credit reporting agencies, where else could lenders turn? Lenddo, an online purveyor of credit in the Philippines is pioneering the use of social media as a means of establishing the credit worthiness of borrowers. Sadly, the idea has taken root on our shores.

Let the Un-friending Begin

When social media begins to play a role in our ability to secure credit, the complexion of social media sites is bound to change. Friends will take on a new significance and you are as likely to be *friended* for your great payment record as you are to be ***un-friended*** for your poor one. It is a brave new world out there … and I think it sucks.

What Would You Do if This Happened to You?

Imagine this for a second. You're busy looking at your friends' and family's latest status updates, and you get friend request from an attractive person. If horror movies are correct, it's the unattractive people that turn out to be psychos so, using wisdom gained from watching endless horror movies you accept the request and go about your business.

A few weeks pass and you noticed this person being more active on your timeline and within your existing pictures. They are commenting frequently and liking all of your stuff. You being the awesome person you are see this as a validation of your awesomeness. After all, who wouldn't like all your pictures and statuses? The people who don't are obviously haters and can't stand your greatness.

Then This Happens...

The attractive person sends you a message in your inbox and follows up with a status update on your wall for the world to see:

"Hey, this is a representative from ABC debt collection agency, we are trying to contact you. Call us when you can!"

Yikes! Now that's embarrassing, but it's legal! Agencies whose job it is to run down consumer debt, aka debt collectors, have been coming under scrutiny lately for doing exactly what I described above.

They have been using Facebook, Twitter, LinkedIn, and all types of social media outlets to get in contact with people who have not responded to formal letters, phone calls, or emails. You may be thinking, "Umm, isn't this an invasion of my privacy?" Well, there is a long answer and a short answer. The short answer is "No." The long answer is "Hell to the no."

You'll find that there are no formal laws in place that say you cannot be contacted via social media by a debt collector. However, there are laws that specify how far a debt collector can go in their efforts to collect. Like, they cannot call you at 10 p.m. or threaten you.

The takeaway here is that social media outlets are PUBLIC INFORMATION. That PUBLIC INFORMATION can and will be used against you in a court of law. Well, in this case when a debt collector is trying to run you down and get paid. I can't wait for the day a debt collector runs up on someone in the supermarket or a restaurant based on the location based status update. Now that would be funny.

As the law currently stands, a debt collector can contact you via social media to request a phone call or email. The good thing is they cannot send your personal information via social media, so if you're contacted at least they won't let your whole timeline know that you owe 10K in medical bills for erectile dysfunction treatments.

With that said, if you own a few debts that are in collections, you should be cautious of who you invite as a friend and what you say on your timeline.

Debt Collectors Calling? Here are 3 Things You Can Do!

If you ever had a debt go into collections, 9 times out of 10 you have debt collectors calling you nonstop. Today, we are going to go over what to do when debt collectors are calling you.

I've had many clients mess up when a debt collector calls them. They get emotional and start saying stuff they aren't supposed to say. So, let's go over the top 3 things you should do when a debt collector calls you.

Tip 1: You need to remember that the phone call is recorded so anything you say will be used against you. I recommend you deny, deny, and deny. Act like you have amnesia!

"Debt? What debt are you referring to? I have to talk to my lawyer about this, can you send something in writing?"

Tip 2: Keep it in writing! Remember that by law the debt collector must provide a validation notice within five days of contacting you. Within 30 days of receiving the debt collector's validation, you should send a written request asking for more details.

You need the written documentation to prove your case, if you have too.

Tip 3: If you don't receive something within five days in the mail advise the collector to stop contacting you and make sure you register with the Do Not Call Registry. According to federal law, a debt collector cannot continue to contact you if you tell them to stop. You can even write them a letter telling them to not contact you anymore. You will want to save a copy of the letter then send the original via certified mail and request a return receipt.

Does Student Loan Debt Hurt Your Credit Score?

As you probably know, your credit score is the result of a complicated calculation. To get to your credit score, the credit bureaus inspect five different areas of your financial situation including:

- **HISTORY**: Do you pay your bills on time, are you always late, never late, that sort of thing.
- **HOW MUCH**: How much money do you owe? More importantly, the credit bureaus want to know how much of your available credit you are using.
- **LENGTH**: Length refers to how long you've had credit (also part of Credit History).
- **NEW CREDIT**: Are you aggressively pursuing new credit cards?
- **TYPE OF CREDIT:** The credit bureaus want to know how much installment debt you have versus how much revolving debt.

Next the credit bureaus collect all of these factors above and feed them into their algorithm. The resulting number is your credit score. Keep this fact in mind—the credit bureaus are trying to assess your credit risk. They only want to determine as accurately as they can if you will or will not pay off a loan.

So, back to our question: *does student loan debt hurt your credit score?*

Sometimes the answer is yes—your student loan debt will hurt your credit score. Then again, in other situations, it will not hurt your credit score. In fact, it may even improve it.

Here's why the true answer is "It depends." Each person's financial situation is different.

First, consider asking the question another way. What if you instead asked: *"How does student loan debt affect my credit report?"* Asking the question this way may help you understand your credit score from the other side.

Remember your student loans are real debt. This means you do owe the money. It also means that your student loan debt will be reported regularly to the credit bureaus, regardless of the status your student loan debt.

Installment Loans versus Revolving Loans

From the perspective of the credit bureau your student loan is considered an installment loan. You may be surprised to learn that installment loans with a very large balance are not considered as bad as a large revolving loan balance. Also, it is important to understand how your student loans are reported. Student loans are reported to the credit bureaus on a disbursement basis. For example, you may have a subsidized loan and a non-subsidized student loan. Each of these loans is reported to the credit bureau as separate loans. This increases both the total amount of debt owed and the number of loans outstanding.

Quick Review

An installment loan is a debt that is repaid over time with a specific number of payments. Examples of installment loans include auto loans, mortgages, and student loans. Revolving loans, on the other hand, don't have a set number of payments, like your credit cards. The point is that installment loan debt balances do not negatively impact your credit score as much as high credit card balances. For example, your student loan debt of $21,975 has less impact on your credit score than your $3,900 Visa card balance.

The Effect on Your Credit Score

The Good: Interestingly, student loan debt can actually improve your credit score. Researchers have even demonstrated that people can have high student loan debt and high credit scores. If you make your payments in full on time, then your credit score can actually improve from your student loan debt. Also, you should note that the entire time you are making payments you are helping yourself establish a credit history.

The Bad: Alternatively, if you miss payments, don't pay the full amount, or worst of all you default on your student loan, then your credit score will be hammered. Defaulting on student loan debt is much worse than defaulting on revolving debt. The reason is due to the nature of student loans. Student loans are set up and administered by federal student loan laws. They cannot be statutorily discharged in a bankruptcy like revolving debt.

Student loan debt absolutely has an impact on your credit score. However, whether the student loan debt increases your credit score or decreases it is largely up to you.

Does Debt Consolidation Ever Make Cents?

If you happen to find yourself on the wrong end of a debt collection call, if you find your mailbox is increasingly filled to the brim with past due notices, if you dread the phone ringing because you just know it may be a debt collector, well then, chances are you are looking for a way out. Not surprisingly, this is exactly the point when quite a few people start looking for outside help.

One option that many find themselves considering at this point is a debt consolidation plan or service. That would seem to be a good logical way to go about it at first glance. But is it? Is debt consolidation really worth considering? Let's take a closer look.

Perhaps the best place to begin is with a clear definition. Unfortunately, there are a lot of terms and phrases thrown around with regards to solving debt problems. Chances are you have across terms such as debt relief, debt settlement plans, debt restructuring and debt consolidation. Sadly, many people use these phrases interchangeably when in fact each of them refers to different options. For this discussion, we will be looking at debt consolidation.

What is Debt Consolidation?

Much like it sounds, debt consolidation means gathering up all (or as much as the plan will allow) your debt and then repackaging this debt as a single new loan with a lower interest rate. In other words, you are taking your pile of bills with multiple monthly payments and interest rates and tying them up all together in one convenient and supposedly easier to handle package. This new bundle (package) allows you to make a single payment, which is then applied to your new consolidated debt loan. On the face of it, it sure looks like a good idea. At least until you read the fine print and understand the real terms associated with a debt consolidation plan. The reality behind debt consolidation may in fact surprise you.

Truth Revealed

Face it; you aren't getting something for nothing. By consolidating your bills into a single loan, you may very well find that you have just stretched your payment term into a much longer payoff period. Not only that, once you factor in the interest over the longer term, you will find that you end up actually paying more over time.

Depressing Statistic

There is yet another fact that might make you look at other options. Industry insiders report that a ridiculously high percentage, like some 78% of clients who use debt consolidation plans to pay off their credit cards, end up racking up even more debt on their credit cards than when they first started. Ouch! Talk about a smack upside the head. Can you imagine paying a debt consolidation loan and still struggling to pay your monthly credit card bill? Ugh!

Can Debt Consolidation Make Cents?

Yes, absolutely. The use of a debt consolidation plan or loan can actually be a great strategy. But debt consolidation really only works if you are in the position to pay off a lot of debt in a short amount of time. For example, suppose you find yourself with three credit cards, each with a balance of around $2,700. You decide you have had enough of the credit card companies and their usurious interest rates and vow to take decisive action. You consolidate all of your credit card debt into a single loan and begin making payments immediately. There's more. Not only do you make payments, you cut up at least two, if not all of your credit cards. Do you see how that works? You won't use the card anymore, and you aren't canceling. Typically, you don't want to cancel a credit card since it will shorten your credit history and could negatively affect your credit.

Easy Button?

Unfortunately debt consolidation is not the Easy Button to end your financial issues. If you find yourself looking at debt consolidation as an option, this is a clue. In other words, something is out of whack in your financial life. Yes, debt consolidation can be a good idea. But then again, it is *not* a quick fix.

Consider your Habits

What are your habits with money and debt? Do you find yourself earning $10 and spending $12? That's a clue. Fix that! Yes, debt consolidation can help you recover from the damage of poor financial habits, but it won't fix the real problem. In other words, lousy personal financial habits are like weeds in your garden. Sure, you cut them out. But then they just come right back. You haven't uprooted the source of the problem.

In the end consolidation may or may not be a good choice for you. Either way, if you're in debt, take the time to learn about debt consolidation and how it could work for you if you were to use it and make positive changes in your personal financial habits at the same time.

What is Better for My Credit Score? A Foreclosure or a Short Sale?

Look twice, decide once, and make sure you know the real facts before you choose one option over another. Although some homeowners consider them remarkably similar, a short sale is not the same as a foreclosure, especially when you are talking about your credit score.

As you probably know, many homeowners are experiencing financial hardships and having more trouble staying in their current homes. Since late 2009, the number of short sales and foreclosures has been increasing. Consequently, more and more people are questioning which option will have the least impact on their credit score. It is essential to understand the meanings of these terms so you can choose responsibly with full understanding of the implications of your choices.

Credit Score

The credit bureaus examine five things to determine your credit risk. Remember, ultimately they are only forecasting, and they are trying to predict if you will pay off a loan. As a brief review, the five areas that the credit bureaus examine are:

- HISTORY: Do you pay on time, are you always late, never late, that sort of thing.
- HOW MUCH YOU OWE: More importantly, the credit bureaus want to know about your available credit, that is, how much of it you are using. They also look at how much you have left.
- HOW LONG HAVE YOU HAD CREDIT (LENGTH): Note that length is also referred to as credit history.
- NEW CREDIT: Are you aggressively pursuing new credit cards?
- TYPE OF CREDIT: The credit bureaus want to know how much installment debt you have versus how much revolving debt.

Foreclosure

A foreclosure means the bank or other lender takes back the house. This is similar to a car dealer repossessing a car that has not been paid for, and the foreclosure process usually doesn't start unless you have missed three consecutive payments.

Short Sale

A short sale is an agreement between you and the lender. In this case, the lender agrees to take less than the agreed-upon loan amount. Oftentimes the lender does this just to go ahead and sell the property. A short sale is sometimes offered when there is not enough equity in the property to both sell the property and also pay all the selling costs.

The Real Effect on Your Credit Score

Back to the big question: *Does a short sale affect your credit score more or less than a foreclosure?* The answer is that it depends. In most cases, effect is about the same. This surprising truth is straight from the people who brought you the credit score to begin with—Fair Isaac. They created the original FICO score (your credit score). Just look at these guidelines directly from Fair Isaac.

Days Late or Other Event	Effect on Credit Score
30 days or more	40 to 100 points down
90 days or more	70 to 135 points down
Foreclosure or Short Sale	85 to 160 points down
Bankruptcy	130 to 240 points down

Do you see the truth revealed here? Per the original credit score people themselves, the effect on your credit score is about the same. Now, that being said, you will notice that each triggering event has a range of effects on your credit score. The range is where the credit score may be affected more or less by a short sale versus a foreclosure.

The reality is that each person's situation is different. However, here are some scenarios which may impact your credit score.

Scenario 1: Negative Effect of Foreclosures

Foreclosures may have a more negative effect on your credit score, and it really depends on how it shows up on your credit report. For example, if you have been steadily been making your mortgage payments on time, and then suddenly stop, that will have a greater negative effect. To the credit bureau, it will look like three or more negative events (missed payments) plus a foreclosure. Alternatively, if you are in foreclosure without multiple negative events, the negative credit score effect will not be as severe.

Scenario 2: Negative Effect of Short Sales

Short sales have two possible negative effects. First of all, if the lender reports the short sale as a *Settlement*, that is much more negative than a paid in full report. Also, beware that with a short sale, depending on the laws in your particular state, the lender may have to come back after you. It's called a *deficiency judgment*, and it is the difference between the original loan amount and the final amount settled. Ouch, that hurts twice. First, you get dinged for the foreclosure, then again with a deficiency judgment.

Both short sales and foreclosures affect your credit score negatively. However, contrary to popular belief, the actual effect on your credit score is about the same.

Lightning Source UK Ltd.
Milton Keynes UK
UKHW052129181119
353790UK00002B/89/P